An admitted perfectionist, Stirling Moss was famous for beating the best car-driver combinations that Ferrari and other teams could offer, and beating them while driving older cars, some far down on power. Why did a man of his ability and stature drive out-classed cars in the first place? Primarily because he is a fierce nationalist, a British driver first, last and always. He drove his country's Formula 1 cars often throughout his career despite the fact that they rarely matched up.

Moss once said "I always enjoyed playing the underdog role. I raced with passion and I loved the competition. When I raced, the name of the game was to push your car and yourself to the limit. But today the name of the game is simply to win. I always tried to win, naurally, but the race itself was everything. I just loved to get in the car and drive the bastard."

Stirling Moss is one of the truly legendary drivers, and we pay tribute to both him and the Moss family, all of whom played major roles in motorsport history.

Gerry Durnell
Editor & Publisher

Automobile Quarterly

The Connoisseur's Magazine of Motoring
– Today, Yesterday, and Tomorrow –

GERRY DURNELL
Editor & Publisher

KAYE BOWLES-DURNELL
Associate Publisher

JOHN C. DURNELL
Chief Operations Officer, Technical Editor

TRACY POWELL
Managing Editor

ALFRED MORESCHI
Art & Design

GINNY HENDRIX
Customer Service

DEBBIE SISK
Subscriptions

TIFFANY WEBBER
Accounting

AMBER STORM
Research

L. SCOTT BAILEY
Founding Editor and Publisher

Contributing Photographers
CLIVE FRIEND,
CAROLYN HASENFRATZ,
FERDINAND HEDIGER,
MICHEL ZUMBRUNN

Contributing Writers
RANDY BARNETT, KATHY BERRY,
DAVID BURGESS-WISE,
JULIE FENSTER, PATRICK FOSTER,
FERDINAND HEDIGER,
MIKE TAYLOR, JOHN R. WRIGHT

www.autoquarterly.com

Printed in Korea

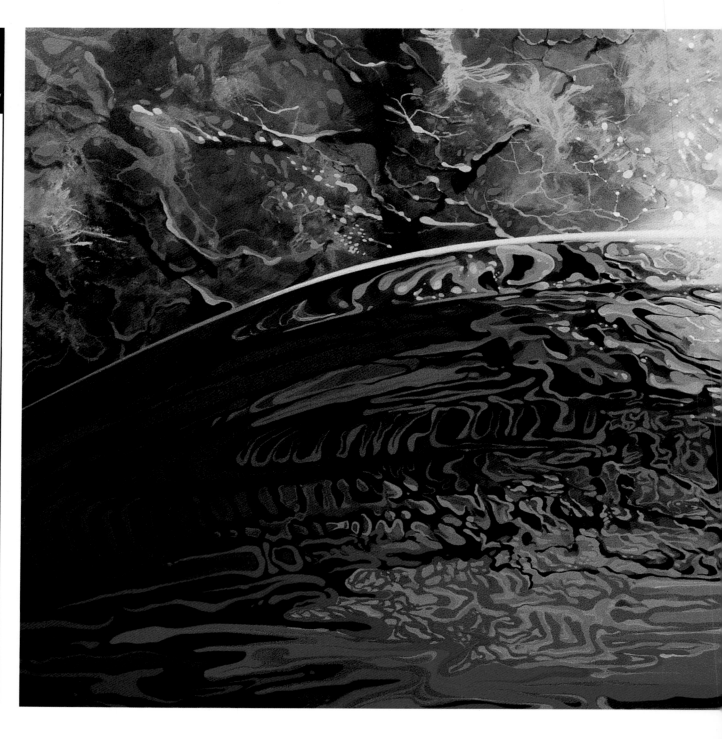

"Viper"

Contents

VOLUME 42, NUMBER 2 • SECOND QUARTER 2002

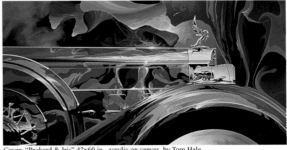

Cover: "Packard & Iris" 42x60 in., acrylic on canvas, by Tom Hale

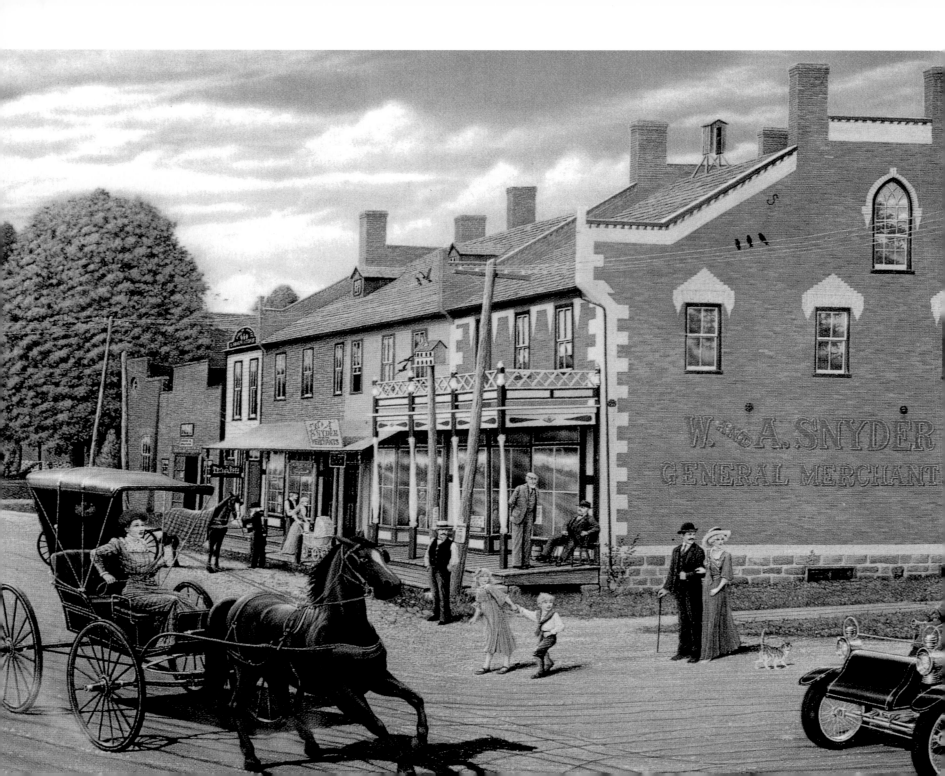

A Canadian Contribution

The LeRoy Automobile

BY JOHN R. WRIGHT

Literally thousands of "would be" and "briefly were" automakers and their companies have come and gone during the approximately 115 years of the automobile. In the case of the Canadian LeRoy automobile, it existed for only a few years and the town where it was built also vanished—or at least its name did.

At the turn of the last century, the city now known as Kitchener, Ontario, was called Berlin. It was well known for its thrifty, hard-working, conservative population. Today, the city boasts 180,000 residents and a strong German heritage. The original town of Berlin was home to the LeRoy automobile built by brothers Milton and Nelson Good. They were assisted by their cousin Isaac "Ike" Neuber.

The Goods' 1902 LeRoy was the first practical full-sized gasoline automobile built in any quantity in Canada, according to Glenn Baechler and Hugh Durnford in their landmark book,

Brothers Milton and Nelson Good

"Cars of Canada."

The two brothers made a good team. Milton Good possessed the inventor's ability to visualize the design of the car and organize the operation, while Nelson Good had the mechanical ability. A third brother, David, although not active in the automobile project, made an important contribution —the new car was named after his son, Leroy. The 1898 prototype built by the brothers and cousin Ike was a high-wheeler, but subsequent vehicles rolled on pneumatic tires obtained from a Dunlop tire distributor in Toronto.

As Milton Good's son Ross recalled: "The story starts on the 6th of October in 1891 when my Uncle Nelson married Margaret Sherriffs of Winterbourne (a small village northeast of Berlin). They then moved into a double brick house near Kaufman's Lumber Mill on King Street.

"My father Milton moved into the other half of the house," Ross said, " in order to build a large workshop for horizontally opposed, water-cooled engines for farm use. Threshing machines, for example."

At this time, there was a major movement to bring mechanized farm machinery to Ontario farmers, machinery such as that produced by the Massey Ferguson Company. The farm industry work by the Good brothers got a boost from Jacob Kaufman, owner of a local lumberyard, when he allowed them to use his premises to make engine patterns when the mill was not in use. Their late night work once proved providential for Kaufman because, as Ross Good said, "On one occasion, a fire started in the shavings, and the brothers put it out. It was a good thing they had been there working on their patterns."

With their knowledge of machinery, Milton and Nelson were determined to build an automobile, but they were not sure how to go about it. Few examples existed around Berlin and there were many variables to consider for the basic design of their car. For early automotive pioneers like the Goods, the designer's drawing board was clean, and all possibilities were open.

In 1897, the brothers saw an advertisement in an American newspaper for

Milton Good's son Ross (above) memorializes his father and uncle's accomplishments on his shed in Wasaga Beach, Ontario.

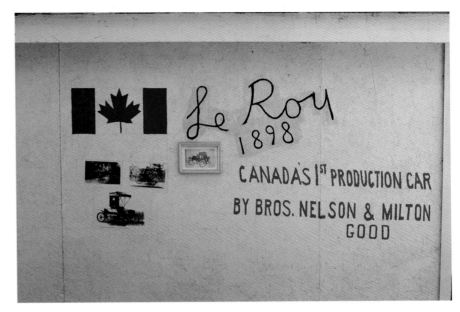

an air-cooled, one-cylinder engine that gave them the idea of building similar short-stroke engines that could be mounted in buggies. As Ross Good recalled: "They built two of these engines as shown in the prototypes, one for Nelson and one for Dad."

Regarding power plants and their design, many early gasoline engine builders were self-taught engineers. Nelson had some experience as an electrician, and Milton had completed some college courses in a technical field, but their engine design arose from practical experience.

Local industries were engaged to do the raw casting work, while the machining of the roughcast blocks was undertaken in the Goods' own workshop. Eventually, the engines were cast of aluminum at the Phillip Foundry, but difficulties arose with the cylinder head and block castings. There were also engine-overheating problems, a common situation with many prototypes of that era, whose engines had a tendency to overheat and seize. As in the case with many other prototypes, the Good brothers did not initially produce a perfect car with a

reliable power plant.

Other problems they faced concerned the basic wheels on the automobile. It soon became obvious to the Goods that the regular buggy wheel would not stand up to the abuse thrust upon it by the powerful, four-horsepower gasoline engine. The rubber rims on the buggy wheels tended to fly off, and the front wheels collapsed on fast turns. So wire wheels, ordered from a local bicycle shop, were tried next. Meanwhile, 28-by-3-inch pneumatic tires were ordered from a Dunlop distributor in Toronto.

Designing a workable and safe steering apparatus was another obstacle to be overcome.

"Father corrected the steering by using lines from the rear center of the back axle—one to each of the front wheels—by using tables of geometry from the book, 'Surveying With Tables (1895),'" said Ross Good. "This book is now on display at the Doon Heritage Crossroads Museum and is signed by

my father."

To prove the reliability of the finished car, Ross Good recalled that Nelson and Milton decided to take a trip to Brown City, Michigan, on September 19, 1900, to visit their brother David at his dairy farm. The 300-mile trip took them three days. On their way west out of Berlin (Kitchener), they passed the small village of New Hamburg. As the brothers drove up a hill just south of the village, they met a farmer in a buggy. Because Milton knew the farmer's horse would panic when it saw this noisy, newfangled vehicle, he grabbed the horse's bridle but was tossed into the air as the animal reared up and back. Milton landed heavily on the ground, with the horse's legs over his backside. The farmer then rode off, roaring with laughter at the woes of the early automobilist.

The pioneering trip was complicated by a number of mechanical glitches, inevitable in any new invention. The engine in the LeRoy prototype would

Wasaga Beach. Ont. Jan 26th 1954

To day I start my 85th Birthday. and hereby verify that this car 1899 Le Roy. made by Good Bro (Nelson & Milton Good of Waterloo & Berlin. Ont.) is now owned by Lionel G. D. Rider. 286 Queen. St Stratford Ont. This the first Canadian car that my brother + myself drove to Brown City Michigan. U.S.A. from Waterloo & Berlin Canada in 1900. It was the first car to cross the U.S.A. boarder from Canada or the U.S.A.

The inspectors at the boarder, asked each others What will we call it? finally one said. machinery

We built the frame in Geo. Hoffman's black smith shop. Waterloo the rest in Kitchener or rather Berlin. In this Shop we were stuck for 3 weeks with the front wheel alinement and I think I have the best. In 1913 I cut off the cross bar 3" of a Winton Six that I owned then.

In 1900 I sent a letter to the Dunlop Tire Co. Toronto. Ont. If they could make 4 Tires + tubes: 28"x3". they said they could if we paid for the moulds. We also had hubs, spokes, and rems to be assembled. The total Bill was 55 $.

The car weight about 950 lbs One Cylinder made by Good Bros, and sold for $250. the speed 12 M.P.H. four horse power. Engine.

Signed Dr Milton H. Good

Wasaga Beach.

Ont.

overheat, seize up and stop every now and then. When the engine was cooled the clearances between the pistons and the cylinder walls would open up and the engine would run again. The two men frequently had to dismantle the engine to tinker with the internals to see if they could reduce the seizing problem. In addition, the dry cell batteries, which provided the spark for the ignition, would lose their charge after about 40 miles, and the Goods would have to install a new set—the prototype had no generator to charge the batteries. A reliable, working electrical system was among the many things the Goods had yet to master. And as if those problems weren't enough, gasoline was hard to find.

After many adventures, the brothers arrived in Sarnia, Ontario, just across the St. Clair River from Port Huron, Michigan. Today, the average motorist breezes over the four-plus lane Blue Water Bridge and across the largest undefended border in the world. In 1900, that famous bridge did not exist, and the international traveler took the ferry across the river.

Clearing customs was different in those days as well, and Canadian customs officials did not know what to make of the brothers' noisy, smelly conveyance. Nor did they know how to classify it. Finally, they allowed the Good brothers on the ferry, but only on condition that they post a $250 bond guaranteeing the return of the automobile—which they labeled "farm machinery"—to Canada. Neither Milton nor Nelson had that much money, and they were stumped until a friendly innkeeper posted the bond for them.

On the way back home to Waterloo County, they traveled at night to prevent the engine from overheating. All went well until they reached the town of St. Mary's (just west of Kitchener), where the car died due to dead batteries. The Good brothers woke up the man in charge of the local powerhouse so they could recharge the batteries and make it home. The Good brothers averaged about 12 miles an hour for the trip to Brown City (not including breakdowns).

After their return home, Milton and Nelson went back to their workshop to see how they could increase the engine's reliability. They disassembled the one-cylinder engine and reduced the diameter of the piston. With that big test over, the Goods decided to gear up for manufacture under their company's new name of "American Motors." A production line was set up at King and Water Streets in Kitchener.

The brothers now altered the design of their cars so sharply that they bore only a slight resemblance to the original prototype. No longer using a high-wheeler design, the cars were lower, sleeker and far more stylish. Indeed, they looked a great deal like the Curved Dash Oldsmobile, which was beginning to capture the public's imagination in the United States. And questions would soon arise as to whether or not the similarity was accidental.

The LeRoy car provided seating for additional passengers with a one-person bench behind the front seat. At the front of the car, meanwhile, where the "bull-nose" curved down, there was a hinge which allowed the entire nose to fold down and form a seat (hopefully a temporary one, because the passengers'

legs would dangle down in front of the car). With no occupant, this compartment could also be used for storage.

Even at the turn of the 20th Century, early manufacturers were aware that the newly arrived motoring public had a need for speed. The Good brothers were well aware of it, and consequently they staged one of the first automobile speed contests in Canadian history. With three of their new cars ready for racing, they competed at a horse track in Preston, a small town just south of Kitchener. Driving that day were Milton and Nelson Good and their cousin Ike Neuber. Among the fans was the loyal lumber yard owner Jacob Kaufman, who said that "These speed demons must have been going at least 20 miles an hour." But Kaufman didn't say who won.

The first LeRoy cars went on sale late in 1901, although some discrepancies exist regarding the exact dates. Patterned after the Curved Dash Oldsmobile, a total of 37 LeRoys were built, making it the first volume production car in Canada.

But the conservative nature of Canadians in general and Berlin (Kitchener) natives in particular meant that the LeRoy would face a rough road where major financing was concerned. And it was here where the Good brothers would have to obtain the bulk of their investment financing.

A year before their cars went on sale, the Good brothers met Ransom Olds when he paid a visit to their shop. There are two versions of the story, and Ross Good's version goes like this: "Ransom Olds called on the

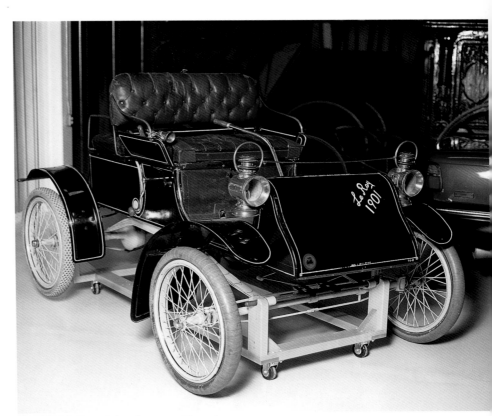

The 1901 LeRoys (above) were patterned after the new Curved Dash Olds produced by Oldsmobile, headed by Ransom Eli Olds (right).

factory in 1900 and drove a LeRoy for the whole day. He was very impressed, and after his test drive the brothers asked him if he would be interested in relocating to Berlin and moving his operation there. But Olds wasn't interested in moving. He needed money, and he wanted it in the form of investment in his company. If Olds couldn't line up investors, he would accept expertise and ideas. He wanted the Goods to move lock, stock and barrel to Detroit. If they did, Olds would enter into a 50/50 partnership with the two brothers.

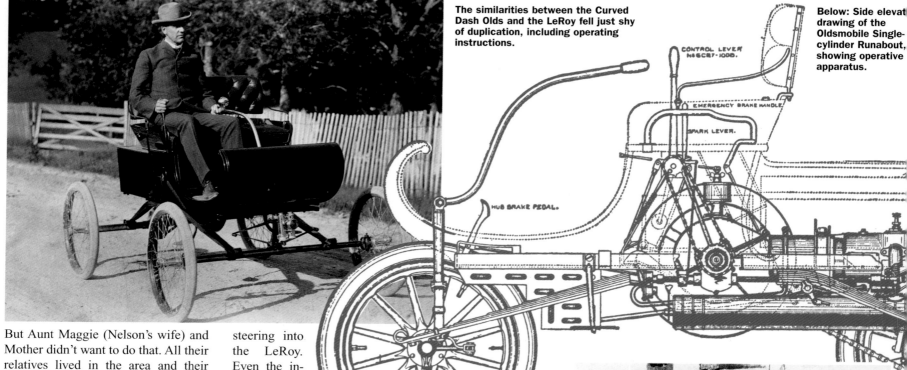

The similarities between the Curved Dash Olds and the LeRoy fell just shy of duplication, including operating instructions.

CONTROL LEVER N86C87-100B.

EMERGENCY BRAKE HANDLE

SPARK LEVER.

HUB BRAKE PEDAL.

Below: Side elevat drawing of the Oldsmobile Single-cylinder Runabout, showing operative apparatus.

The LeRoy M'f g. Co. The Oldest Automobile Firm in Canada.

Manufacturers of The LeRoy Automobile ✳ "Ask the man who owns one."

Berlin, Ont., Aug. 18th 1904

A LeRoy advertisement advises the prospective owner to "Ask the man who owns one."

But Aunt Maggie (Nelson's wife) and Mother didn't want to do that. All their relatives lived in the area and their family ties were strong."

A second version of the Olds story holds that a Mr. Rumpel, an independent businessman (his Rumpel Felt Company is still in operation in the Kitchener area today), brought Olds to the Kitchener area with a view to persuading him to invest in local business, including the Good brothers' American Motors company. What is not revealed in the Good family's history of their car (and what Olds may or may not have known) is that the brothers had purchased a second-hand Curved Dash Olds and stripped it completely. They also built patterns of the Olds engine and copied it. Their problems with the LeRoy's steering were alleviated by adapting a version of the Curved Dash

steering into the LeRoy. Even the instruction booklet for the LeRoy was a direct copy of the Olds booklet. Olds may have been interested in determining how successful a copy the Goods had made of both the car and booklet to see if there had been any copyright or patent infringement. Such infringements could have put a serious crimp in the Goods production of the LeRoy.

The Olds automotive design and instruction booklet were not the only things the Goods appropriated from another company. A LeRoy advertisement from 1904 advises the prospective buyer to "Ask the man who owns one."

Packard had been using this now-famous slogan for quite some time before the Goods adapted it.

Regardless, neither Olds nor Packard ever took legal action, and the Good brothers carried on with their automobile production.

In 1907, LeRoy production ceased after sales continued to fall. The 37 or so cars built during 1899-1907 quickly

disappeared from the roads, leaving only two examples existing today: one in the National Museum of Science and Technology in Ottawa, Ontario, and the other in the Doon Crossroads Heritage Museum in Kitchener. The original high-wheeler—"The Brown City automobile"—was subsequently purchased by Moses Schultzhauer, a Stratford, Ontario, native, for $650. After driving it for some time, he sold it to another owner who dismantled and stored the components in his barn. The car was restored in 1950 by a local auto enthusiast, Lionel Rider, who drove it in parades and on other outings. The LeRoy prototype was donated to the Doon Heritage Museum by another owner, Norman Schneider. In 1954, Milton Good wrote a letter to Rider, describing the trip he and his brother had taken to Michigan and verifying the authenticity of the high-wheeler.

Why did the LeRoy fail? Lack of investment was the main reason, plus many mechanical problems along the way. Frankly, the LeRoy was not a very good automobile, thanks to a lack of planning. No hard research outside traditional rules of thumb had been done to produce a reliable working car.

For example, the Good brothers never really solved the problem of brakes. One stopped the car by stamping on the pedal that controlled the planetary transmission. Worse yet, the LeRoy had no reverse gear as such. If a motorist wanted to back up, he stopped the car by stamping on the clutch pedal, turning off the engine, and then pushing the car backwards.

In any case, the LeRoy's engineering and technical problems, which might have been solved by an infusion of money and good engineering, were not resolved. By this time, automotive innovation had taken another leap forward,

and the Good brothers had only managed to construct a basic vehicle that moved under its own power. Meanwhile, the North American market was ready for low-priced cars built at a rate that would accommodate the masses. For example, in 1907, when the LeRoy folded, there were only 2,130 automobiles in Canada. By 1912, there were more than 50,000. In such a growth market, the Good brothers could not have survived with their limited production facilities.

Perhaps another reason for failure came when Milton and Nelson got bored with the idea of producing an automobile and decided to go on to other things.

Of course, the LeRoy's resemblance to the Curved Dash Oldsmobile—a popular car which had greater resources behind it—may have contributed to the fall as well.

After the 1907 demise of their automobile, the Good brothers remained in business for a short time by selling stationary engines for farm use, but business was slow. Eventually, the patterns for the LeRoy engine were sold to Gilson Manufacturing of Guelph, Ontario. Milton went on to graduate from an American academy in osteopathy and became a respected osteopath, treating many local people during his long career in that field. He died in 1955, 41 years after his brother Nelson's death in 1914.

Long after the fact, it is difficult to measure the Good brothers' contribution to the Canadian auto industry. One thing is certain, however. The Goods were wholly Canadian producers of a Canadian automobile, and they relied

Partial reason behind LeRoy's failure in 1907 can be attributed to the promotional resources found at direct competitor Oldsmobile.

primarily on home-grown technology—augmented by borrowed American expertise—to produce their cars. They were also the first to build automobiles commercially outside of Ontario's major manufacturing center, Toronto.

Like so many pioneers of the motoring age, Milton and Nelson Good weren't afraid to embrace untried concepts or risk their slender capital. Their company may have failed, but not before the brothers pursued their dream of creating and building their very own automobile. ▲◎

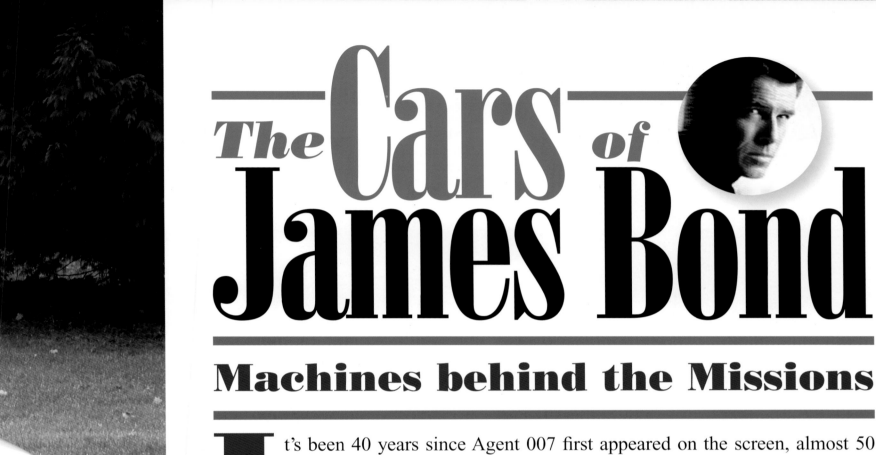

The Cars of James Bond

Machines behind the Missions

It's been 40 years since Agent 007 first appeared on the screen, almost 50 since novelist Ian Fleming wrote the first James Bond novel. And in the increasingly gadget-filled world of Bond, fast cars—and in particular Aston Martins—continue to play a central role.

They call it the most famous car in the world, but the maker of the Aston Martin DB5 first driven by British secret agent James Bond in the 1964 movie "Goldfinger" wasn't keen for it to be used in the film of Ian Fleming's novel, recalled Oscar-winning set designer Ken Adam when I interviewed him at his London home.

"When we started work on 'Goldfinger', the producers, Cubby Broccoli and Harry Saltzman, were discussing with me what sort of car Bond should drive. They didn't want him to go back to Ian Fleming's Green Label Bentley, so we decided to give him the most sexy British sports car of the period, which was the Aston Martin.

"I remember contacting David Brown (owner of Aston Martin), and he wasn't all that enthusiastic about supplying us with a couple of Astons, so I left the negotiations to the two producers. After

BY DAVID BURGESS-WISE

13

the success of the film, Aston Martin sales went up by—I believe—60 percent, and after that we never had any problems with people letting us have cars for the Bond films!"

Films often diverge from the novels they are based on—and that's been increasingly true of the Bond movies. But in the case of "Goldfinger", at least the marque of Agent "007" Bond's car remained constant, for novelist

deep hatred of the Nazis inspired him to volunteer as a pilot when Britain went to war against Germany in 1939.

Powered by the fearsomely complex 24-cylinder H-formation sleeve-valve Napier Sabre engine, the 2200 hp Typhoon was the most powerful piston-engined fighter to serve against the Third Reich. It could exceed 400 mph in level flight. And it had a lethal sting.

"The Typhoon was the ultimate rocket

"Our losses were terrifying—flying from 8,000 to zero feet, we were very exposed to the German flak—and I'm very lucky to still be around. But it was all great fun."

Indeed, you can sense that Adam—trained as an architect—got much of the inspiration for the ultimate fate of the spectacular sets he created for seven classic Bond films from his wartime activities. A wartime history of the

close to me," he admits.

Adam sketched out a range of lethal fitments for Bond's DB5. Apart from the ejector seat, it had .303-caliber Browning machine guns hidden behind the retractable sidelights, a rear oil slick, wheel-shredding extending hubnuts, revolving license plates, a bulletproof shield for the backlight and spiked caltrops that could be dropped in the path of a pursuing vehicle to puncture its

Fleming had given him an Aston DB Mk III. However, the panoply of gadgets fitted to the film's DB5 was based on Adam's wartime experiences flying Hawker Typhoons for the Royal Air Force. And, as Ken Adam—born Klaus Adam in Berlin in 1921—told me, he was probably the only German citizen to fly for the RAF. His family had been forced to leave his homeland after Hitler came to power in 1933, and his

fighter," said Adam. "It had eight rockets whose warheads had the explosive power of a six-inch naval shell, backed up by four 20mm Hispano cannons. It was such a powerful weapon that we were attached to the 2nd Tactical Air Force, providing the Canadian and British Armies with most effective air support from D-Day onwards.

Typhoon details its favorite targets as "flak-towers, gasometers, locomotives, rolling stock, mechanical transport and aircraft dispersed on the ground." Sounds just like the finale of a typical Bond film.

And it was Adam's flying experiences that prompted his creation of the Bond DB5's most famous accessory, the ejector seat: "World War II was still pretty

tires. His special effects engineers, vintage motorcycle enthusiast Johnny Stears ("the Dean of F/X") and Bert Luxford, "made it all happen."

The gadgets, said Adam, were a kind of surrogate revenge on careless drivers for damage to his beloved Jaguar XK-E coupe: "Every time I parked it, it seemed as though the front was dented.

"We very rarely resorted to tricking things up in the Bond films I was involved with," he told me, "because we felt it was being dishonest with the audience. Most of the time we did things for real, like the famous

'Thunderball' jet pack."

His extras for the film's DB5s—two apparently converted, including the ex-DB4 DB5 prototype BMT 216A—even forecast a gadget that would not become reality for several decades—a tracker device concealed in the fascia that located the target vehicle on a tiny TV screen.

The gadgets developed by the eccentric weapons expert "Q" (played by veteran actor Desmond Llewellyn) were for cinema Bond: in Fleming's novels Bond most memorably drove "a battered gray Bentley." Even in the mid-

Landing on the mysterious Crab Key, Bond (Sean Connery) meets Honeychile Ryder (Ursula Andress) in the first Bond film, "Dr No." The DB5 (opposite) was yet to come.

1950s when Fleming endowed Bond with the Bentley, it was an unorthodox choice of everyday transport, particularly for someone in Bond's cloak-and-dagger profession where anonymity was a virtue. And Fleming was most particular about what kind of Bentley: "A 4.5-liter Bentley with an Amherst-Villiers super-charger (please note the solid exactitude)," he wrote in 1962.

Doubtless that stirred memories for Fleming, who in the interwar years had, like Bond, "dabbled in motor sport." Writing in his "Atticus" column in 1954, he recalled: "The first time I traveled at 100 mph on the open road was in a 3-liter Bugatti along the Fair Mile at Henley in 1928."

Fleming was probably at Le Mans in 1930, for in his 1955 novel "Moonraker" he writes of Bond "hearing again the harsh scream of Caracciola's great white beast of a car as it howled past the grandstands." The German "Regenmeister" only raced at Le Mans once, and that was the year, of course, that Caracciola's Mercedes was hounded by "Tim" Birkin's supercharged Bentley till it broke. The gallant performance of the Blower Bentley would have impressed the 22-year-old Fleming (he must have been writing about himself, for in 1930, according to the fictional Bond's timeline, the future "007" would have been just 5 years old).

And in "Moonraker", too, Fleming wrote of Bond watching the Grand Prix Mercedes of the '30s at Tripoli and Berne "with the Auto Unions on their tails."

In August 1932, when Fleming was working as a stringer for a press agency, he covered the Alpine Rally as navigator for Donald Healey, who won the event in an S-Type 4.5-liter Invicta without incurring a single penalty. That won Healey a coveted Coupe des Glaciers and a flight in the "Graf Zeppelin" for his team.

But as a successful novelist, Fleming's personal cars were relatively tame: in 1954 he bought an Armstrong Siddeley, a couple of years later came a Ford

"Goldfinger" saw the debut of Bond's Aston DB5. This one was actually the prototype and had started life as a DB4.

Thunderbird.

Even the film cars began modestly: In the first Bond film, the 1962 "Dr. No", Bond drove a Sunbeam Alpine—a milquetoast 1.6-liter sports car based on the humble Hillman Minx family sedan—which was involved in 007's first screen car chase, ending when the hoodlums' hearse crashed over a cliff in flames.

Nor did Bond get much motoring in during the next film, "From Russia with Love", released in 1963. Maybe it's because Ken Adam didn't work on this one—he was involved with Stanley Kubrick's "Dr. Strangelove"—and production design was handled by his assistant on "Dr. No", Syd Cain. Nevertheless, once again a Bond gadget was considerably ahead of reality, though it was nothing more lethal than a car-

phone fitted in his classic Bentley.

A year later came "Goldfinger". Ken Adam was back, the sets and special effects were outstanding—some say the best ever—and the famed Aston DB5 made its debut. The chase round Auric Goldfinger's secret factory, in which the ejector seat is deployed to deadly effect, was actually filmed around the grim pro-

duction buildings at Pinewood Studios in rural Buckinghamshire, home of the early Bond films. There was also villain Auric Goldfinger's notorious Rolls-Royce Phantom III, with its solid gold body panels concealed by paint—a foolproof method of bullion smuggling—and his impassive Korean servant Oddjob's lethal bowler hat!

But it wasn't a razor-edged hat but his fast-lane lifestyle that cut down Ian Fleming during the filming of "Goldfinger". After years of butter-rich food, smoking and drinking, he suffered a massive heart attack in 1964 while visiting the Royal St. George's golf course at Sandwich in Kent. He was only 56.

Goldfinger's Phantom III (top) was literally worth its weight in gold. After "You Only Live Twice" was filmed, production designer Syd Cain bought the white Toyota 2000GT (bottom) and was booked for going through a police speed trap at 140 mph. Right: Ken Adam with his Typhoon in tow.

Bond's glamorous Japanese aide Aki (Akiko Wakabayashi). The highly publicized Toyota filled the bill, and two were ordered from Japan. The only snag was that the car was only available as a fixed-head coupe—and the script called for a convertible.

Undaunted, Broccoli called on the metalworking talents of Veteran Car Club member John Mitchell, who had built many "specials" for film work. He duly created a drivable 2000GT convertible equipped with the "Q"-developed "extras"—in this case rocket launchers—demanded of any self-respecting Bond-mobile.

At this point the steady production sequence of the Bond films was interrupted by a difference of focus between producers Saltzman and Broccoli, with each working on a pet project for 1968. Harry Saltzman made the epic "Battle of Britain" while Broccoli produced a musical based on "Chitty-Chitty-Bang-Bang", a whimsical children's book by Ian Fleming about a magical flying car (inspiration came from the World War I song that

Next in the film canon was "Thunderball". The DB5 reprised its role, and for good measure Adam drew on his Typhoon experience to create a rocket-firing motorbike for villainess Fiona Volpe, who used it to blow away the big Ford of failed SPECTRE agent Count Lippe. Ford of Britain, which had supplied the US-built car via its Lincoln

Cars subsidiary, took advantage of the loan to make a comedy short entitled "A Child's Guide to Blowing Up a Motor Car" fronted by comedy writer Denis Norden.

Producers Cubby Broccoli and Harry Saltzmann, who had formed Eon Pictures to film the Bond novels, then made "You Only Live Twice". This

movie didn't have a lot of room for cars, though it did introduce the memorable packaway autogyro "Little Nellie" (see sidebar). But there was one notable automobile in the film—a very special Toyota 2000GT, a unique example of arguably the first supercar to be built by the Japanese motor industry.

Broccoli wanted a suitable car for

slighted Count Louis Zborowski's aero-engined cars of the 1920s).

I did some technical advisory work on this film's opening sequence, which featured a number of fictitious motor races set in Edwardian days: it reunited several members of the Bond production team, including designer Ken Adam and metalworking wizard John Mitchell, who built a number of looka-like racing cars and made all the brass-work for the several Chitties used in filming.

Recalled Adam: "Chitty-Chitty-Bang-Bang turned out to be one of the most complicated things I'd ever done. Chitty-Chitty-Bang-Bang had to look like a period car. I'd always been fascinated by the radiator of the early Bugattis, so I decided to use a similar sort of front to the car and then design a boat body based on some of the old Rollses for the rest of the car."

A relentless perfectionist, Adam "drove everybody crazy" at Pinewood Studio until he was satisfied with the design. But the first Chitty-Chitty-Bang-Bang, with its wooden skiff body constructed by a Thames boatbuilder, brought the entire studio to a standstill, said Adam: "It was an interesting and rather beautiful-looking car—the finish was fabulous."

Saltzman and Broccoli were back together for the next Bond film, "On Her Majesty's Secret Service", made in 1969. Missing was Sean Connery, whose laconic delivery had created the arche-typal screen Bond. His replacement—for one film only—was George Lazenby, a former male model, and Aston Martin's role was reduced to a drive-on one, this time for the chunky new DBS. The

Bond's Lotus Esprit Turbo from "The Spy who Loved Me" not only sprayed cement at pursuing cars but transformed into a submarine armed with rockets, limpet mines, an underwater smoke screen and surface-to-air missiles!

action role went to a red Ford Cougar convertible "owned" by heroine Contessa Tracy di Vicenzo (Diana Rigg), which outran the hoodlums' cars and even got involved in a Swiss ice race with Ford Escorts. Ford's Film Unit again capitalized on this connection by issuing a documentary entitled "Shot on Ice".

Connery was back in the next Bond

movie, "Diamonds Are Forever", but the "star car" this time was a '71 Ford Mustang that performed spectacular stunts on the streets of Las Vegas in a chase with police cars. Doubling for Bond at the wheel was stuntman Buzz Bundy, who performed a memorable two-wheel slither down a Vegas alley-way. Inevitably, the pursuing car failed to make it!

Apart from that, the main motorized interest was an Adam-designed "Moon Buggy" used by Bond to break out of the White Technology Center in the Nevada desert.

Cars played a secondary role in the next Bond film, too. "Live and Let Die" of 1973 marked the debut of Roger Moore (the former TV "Saint") in the Bond role, Connery having announced

that he would never play Bond again (but "never" proved to be just 12 years). The most exciting automotive stunt in this movie occurred when Bond, having hijacked a double-decker bus to get away from drug baron Kananga, drives under a low bridge and amputates the bus's top.

A year later came "The Man with the Golden Gun"—the last Bond picture in which Harry Saltzman was involved—and this time flying cars were all the rage. Villain Scaramanga escaped police pursuit in his Rolls Royce by attaching wings and a jet engine. But the "star" Bond car was, of all unlikely things, an AMC Hornet, which first took to the skies without wings when Bond, using a broken bridge as a take-off ramp, barrel-rolled it across a river. This 360-degree mid-air rollover was a reprise of the famed "Astro Spiral" stunt devised by scientists at the Calspan Laboratories in Buffalo, New York.

The plot called for Bond to steal this car from a car rental agency. Curiously, wings were later fixed to the Hornet to enable it to fly away to safety, not a fea-ture normally included in a rental agreement!

Ken Adam's passion for fast cars saw a new marque—Lotus—make its debut in the next Bond film, "The Spy Who Loved Me" (1977). Adam told me: "I'd known Colin Chapman for some time. I owned a Lotus, which overall was not a success. It was built like a racing car—great for road-holding and speed, but something was always going wrong."

Nevertheless, a Lotus Turbo Esprit became Bond's car of choice. Equipped with a self-destruct mechanism, the Esprit was powered by a 360-hp twin turbocharged four-cylinder engine capable of propelling it to a maximum of 165 miles per hour. Department Q had worked its magic on the Lotus, which could transform itself into a small submarine, complete with radar screen, periscope, underwater smoke-screen, surface-to-air missile and har-poon gun.

"The Spy Who Loved Me" adventure was filmed on the Costa Smeralda on the Mediterranean island of Sardinia. In one scene Bond is pursued by steel-toothed, 7-foot 2-inch villain "Jaws," who drives a Ford Cortina. It plunges over a cliff and through the roof of a cottage, from which Jaws duly emerges unscathed. Later on, Ford used the Costa Smeralda for a product launch, and driving to the hotel I was amused to see that the little cottage which had been portrayed in the film as being at the bot-tom of a valley was actually at the top of a hill.

Elsewhere in the film Bond is pur-sued by an assassin riding a Kawasaki Z900 motorbike with a rocket-equipped sidecar, but Bond manages to outdrive him.

For "The Spy Who Loved Me" the inventive Adam created a supertanker whose bows opened to swallow sub-marines. What he didn't know was that the U.S. Navy base in Sardinia was home port to just such a "mother ship." Its hull contained a dock whose under-water entrance enabled submarines to come and go unobserved.

"Moonraker", released in 1979, was the last Bond film for which Ken Adam was production designer, but cars took a back seat to fast boats and space shut-tles in this one.

In the 1981 "For Your Eyes Only", 007's multi-talented white Lotus com-mitted hara-kiri by blowing itself up with its own anti-theft device, so he had to ride in the Citroën 2CV of Bond Girl Melina Havelock. The 2CV got some-what reshaped in the ensuing action. Later in the film, Bond switched to another Lotus Esprit—this time a cop-per-colored one fitted with ski racks.

In 1983 came the "unofficial" "Never Say Never Again", in which Connery redonned his toupee to make a one-film comeback as Bond. The film featured Bond's first love, the Bentley marque—this time a delicious 1937 three-position drophead Derby Bentley—plus some nifty motorbike riding by lady terrorist Fatima Blush.

Confusingly, Roger Moore reap-peared the same year as Bond in Eon's "Octopussy". In this one, 007 comman-deers a Mercedes and, having lost his tires in a chase, takes to the railroad tracks to pursue a train. Also appearing in a largely carless film are "Tuk-Tuk" taxis cars—Alfa Romeo GTV6s.

In 1985 Roger Moore played Bond for the last time. The film was "A View to a Kill" and again, the car interest was slight, unless you count the little Renault 11 that Bond commandeers from a taxi driver to chase the murder-ous May Day. He then manages to com-prehensively trash it through watching May Day—who is overhead in a para-chute—rather than the road ahead. The car was actually handled by celebrated French stunt driver Remy Julienne, who had also worked on "Octopussy".

The well-armed V8 used in the 1987 Bond film "The Living Daylights" marked the revival of the "super rela-tionship" between Aston Martin and the filmmakers.

The next Bond film, "The Living Daylights", not only featured a new, younger, Bond—43-year-old Timothy Dalton —but saw the return of Aston Martin to the series. And not just one Aston, but two, a Volante convertible (Aston Martin boss Victor Gauntlett's own car) and a standard V8. The armory fitted to the car by "Q"—still played by the aged Desmond Llewellyn—was impressive. It had guided missiles con-cealed behind the fog lamps and aimed by a computerized head-up aiming dis-play projected on the windshield, retractable snow spikes in the tires, deadly laser beam cutters, retractable

B549 WUU

Bond's 1987 Aston Martin V8 featured accessories not normally supplied by Newport Pagnell, like stinger missiles concealed behind the fog lights and deadly laser beams in the wheel hubs, plus retractable spikes in the tires and skis in the sills augmented by a rocket booster in the tail to allow the Aston to travel rapidly over ice and snow.

skis and a rocket booster in the tail. Plus the now traditional self-destruct system (though the cars that were destroyed in the film were highly detailed fiberglass replicas, apart from the bumpers, windows and windshields—so many were used that private owners faced a temporary shortage).

Not only did Broccoli and Saltzman borrow Gauntlett's Volante for 007—the film showed it being "converted" into a

Dalton's second—and final—Bond film was the 1989 "Licence to Kill", in which, apart from Wayne Newton's stretch limo, the vehicles were merely used—and destroyed—as spectacular stunt props, notably the sequence where three giant gasoline trucks are chased down a twisting mountain road by a helicopter and a light aircraft.

Then came a long pause in the regular sequence of Bond movies. When the

series "Remington Steele". Hailed by many as the best Bond since Connery, Brosnan made a graceful bow to tradition by appearing at the wheel of an Aston DB5, this one subtly bearing the British registration "BMT 214A" against the "BMT 216A" that appeared on the revolving license plate of the "Goldfinger" Aston. By amazing coincidence, the "GoldenEye" DB5 was chassis #1484, just two earlier than the

against the red Ferrari 355GTS of the evil Janus Crime Syndicate agent Xenia Onatopp. The Aston won!

But Bond's "Q-Car" in this film was a bullet-proof BMW Z3 Roadster which—though fitted with stinger missiles, rear parachute, radar and SATNAV tracking—played only a very minor role. It smacked more of product placement than gung-ho Bond action, a role which bizarrely was reserved for a Soviet T-55

Bond's "GoldenEye" DB5, prepared by Aston Martin experts Stratton Motor Company, poses with the "clones" prepared as doubles for filming.

Current James Bond Pierce Brosnan and the DB5 used in "GoldenEye", in which a champagne chiller and fax machine replaced the ejector seat of the original.

hardtop V8 by Department "Q"—but they even suggested that he play a KGB general. Sadly for Aston fans, Gauntlett had to turn down the offer as he was too busy turning the ailing Aston Martin Lagonda company around. (The turnaround was aided by Cubby Broccoli, who—at the age of 78—bought himself a new Volante convertible to use in California.)

next in the series, "GoldenEye", appeared in 1995, there was yet another James Bond, Irish-born Pierce Brosnan, who had first come to popular notice in the title role of the long-running TV

original "Goldfinger" car, chassis #1486.

Changing times saw the DB5 equipped with a fax machine and champagne holder. It was not used as a stunt car but demonstrated its prowess in a race on French roads

Battle Tank in which Bond chased the Zil limousine of General Ourumov through the streets of St. Petersburg, seemingly demolishing much of the former Russian capital in the process.

Happily, the BMW 750iL used by Bond in "Tomorrow Never Dies"—the second "Brosnan" film and the first to be released after the death of Cubby

Bond's BMW 750iL (opposite) from "Tomorrow Never Dies" featured rockets in the sunroof and a 20,000-volt defense screen to deter intruders. In the same film the BMW R1200C motorbike (above left) was ridden in a daring rooftop chase through Saigon by stuntman Jean-Pierre Goy, who even jumped the rotor blades of a pursuing helicopter. The titanium-bodied BMW Z8 (above right) was cut in half by giant sawblades attached to the villain's whirlybird in "The World is not Enough."

Broccoli in June 1996—was not only packed with gadgets, but used them.

This time the handover took place in a Munich car rental agency, where "Q" demonstrated the most useful "optional extra" on Bond's BMW—remote control through 007's mobile phone. Other unusual features included a wire-cutter in the hood, impact-proof glass, a dozen stinger missiles, re-inflating tires, theft-proofing by electric-shocking bodywork and that old favorite, tire-puncturing caltrops ejected from the rear of the car. But the car was written off in a high-altitude return through the front window of the car rental store.

BMW really got its share of the action in this movie, for Bond and his Chinese lady sidekick escaped the pursuing bad guys in an amazing rooftop chase shackled together on a BMW R1200C motor bike.

Released in 1999, the last Bond movie of the 20th Century took its title "The World Is Not Enough" from the Bond family motto. It was 85-year-old Desmond Llewellyn's last appearance as "Q" before his tragic death in a car accident. He had, incidentally, appeared in 17 Bond films, more than any other actor. However the succession was assured by introducing John Cleese as his equally batty assistant "R", who aided "Q" in creating another lethally equipped BMW Roadster, this time a Z8 complete with armor-plating, a missile launcher and—again—remote control. Which didn't save it from being bisected by a giant circular saw just like Laurel and Hardy's Model T.

In August 2001 it was announced that the three-film flirtation with the BMW marque had been a temporary one and that for "Die Another Day", the twentieth Bond film in the Eon franchise, Agent 007 will be back at the wheel of an Aston Martin. Provisionally titled "Beyond the Ice", this latest Bond adventure will feature the very latest high-tech Aston, the $228,000 V12 Vanquish, whose body is a sensuous blend of aluminum and carbon fiber.

What deadly gadgets will "Q"'s successor incorporate in the Vanquish? That's guesswork at present, and Aston Martin boss Dr. Ulrich Bez isn't giving

Bond may be "licensed to kill, not to break the speed limit," but the temptation to speed will surely be there with his latest wheels of choice, the Aston Martin Vanquish. For the twentieth Bond film "Die Another Day"(due for release in December 2002), the Vanquish—finished in the same shade of silver as the "Goldfinger" DB5—has been re-engineered to take the 4x4 drivetrain of a V8 Ford Explorer for a spectacular duel with a Jaguar XK8 on a frozen lake.

anything away when he says: "James Bond will find the Aston Martin Vanquish technologically advanced and perfectly suited for the type of work he does today. It combines elements from our heritage, but also clearly shows the direction of the company's future."

But it's bound to add up to the immortal words of "Q": "Don't touch that button, Bond!" AQ

24

Bond in the Air

Little Nellie: an interview with its creator

It wasn't fun making a Bond film," recalls Wing Commander Ken Wallis, who—doubling for 007—flew his remarkable autogyro "Little Nellie" in some of the most memorable action sequences in "You Only Live Twice."

"At times it was really hair-raising. I was flying over an active volcano, which blew its top from time to time, and taking off and landing on gravel cliff edges. And when I'd slithered to a stop on the brink, they'd say, 'We had trouble with No. 2 camera, can you do that again?'

"I did a total of 85 flights—46 hours in the air—for 7 minutes on screen."

At age 85, Wallis still pilots his autogyros with aplomb, but his interest in flying goes way back: "My father and

uncle built a plane in 1910," he said, "and in the 1930s I watched Henri Mignet demonstrate his Flying Flea. Its small scale appealed to me, and I started building one. But I hadn't gotten very far when the design was banned after a series of accidents. Then I bought a two-seat glider for 30 shillings ($7.00 USD), but found it such a business to attach the wings before I could fly it."

During war service with the Royal Air Force, Wallis became aware of German experiments with light rotary-wing aircraft, and in 1956, when he was posted on assignment to Strategic Air Command in the United States, he saw plans for a rotary-winged device known as the Bensen Gyroglider and wondered how a powered version would perform.

"I knew about lightweight engines from my experience with airscrew boats."

He returned to Britain in 1958 and built his first powered autogyro—"I was thrilled when it flew across the field"—but realized the flaws in the concept. Inspired by the military potential of a one-man autogyro, Wallis started again with a clean sheet of paper.

Eventually, his exploits got him an invitation to fly one of his autogyros in a "Spaghetti Bond" film made in Brazil by Italians. A radio interview about the trip prompted an invitation to Pinewood Studios from former RAF colleague Hamish Mahaddie, who had become aviation consultant to Eon Productions, and so "Little Nellie" was born.

"That film business about packing

'Little Nellie' into Louis Vuitton suitcases was a pure gimmick," smiles Wallis. "When I took 'Nellie' abroad, I just removed her rotors and loaded her into the hold of a Boeing 707."

As perhaps the most practical of all the Bond vehicles, Nellie needed no special effects trickery in the flying scenes: "The helicopter pilots would ask me to slow up, as they couldn't keep up with Nellie," says Wallis. "She could run rings round them."

Filming in Japan ended after a mid-air collision cost ace aerial cameraman John Jordan a leg. "We did the rest of the filming over the Sierra Nevada in Spain. And anyway the Japanese wouldn't allow us to fire rockets over their Mount Sakurajima national park."

Carrosserie

Mercedes-Benz 680S Torpédo transformable 1929

Bodies by Saoutchik

The outstanding and elegant transformables, cabriolets, coupés and town cars of Jacques Saoutchik for many years represented the essence of Parisian chic. They regularly were distinguished by collecting awards and prizes in the cherished Concours d'Elégances of Paris and the fashionable resorts at the Atlantic coast and the Côte d'Azur.

BY FERDINAND HEDIGER

It was a violent world in the village close to the Bielo-Russian capital Minsk which greeted Iakov Saoutchik on his birth in 1880. Farmers and craftsmen had been eternally reduced to servitude by the despotic nobility. But finally, the Russians, living in bondage and gloomy anger, revolted. The little boy, son of Jewish parents, who stemmed from the Ukraine, was not quite one year old when the czar was killed in an assault. This, however, did not improve the situation of the poor people and their burden became even heavier.

The new ruler, Czar Alexander III, tried with an iron fist to regain all the privileges and rights for the feudalistic upper class of land-lords and aristocracy. He decreed oppression, expulsion and even elimination of the revolutionists as well as the religious minorities, and agreed to the cruel programs against the Jews. Thus the childhood and youth of Iakov Saoutchik was coined not only by fear and worry, but also by the strong will and self-assurance to overcome problems. After his school years he started an apprenticeship as a cabinetmaker.

Apparently the young man had learned about the fast progress in the world of Western Europe. In 1899, at the age of 19, he left Russia, which was again suffering from new outbreaks of violence and a serious economic crisis. Together with his mother, brothers and sisters he reached Paris. Vladimir Ilitch Ulianov (later much better known by

J. SAOUTCHIK

Double Phaéton " arrière démontable " pouvant être avantageusement remplacé par LIMOUSINE " LANDAULET " et même par " pointe de course " avec siège invisible.

Above: Earliest known Saoutchik sales folder, circa. 1908
Left: Jacques Saoutchik

the name of Lenin) had just published his book "The Development of Capitalism in Russia." Under the adapted name "Jacques," Saoutchik and a French craftsman opened a humble workshop as cabinetmakers in the 11th district of Paris.

A thriving center of trade, industry and engineering, Paris offered the young and eager Russian Jacques Saoutchik many possibilities and opportunities. The automobile, which was becoming more and more fashionable, fascinated him. The cartwrights, wheelwrights, upholstery workers and

lacquer craftsmen—in brief, the coachbuilders—found a completely new and promising field of activity.

In 1906, Jacques Saoutchik got married and founded his own coachbuilding company in Neuilly, an up-and-coming industrial suburb of Paris. As the French automobile historian Serge Bellu wrote, he built his first body on the chassis of an Isotta-Fraschini.

Without a doubt, he wanted to cater to the top class. At that time, car-bodies still had much in common with the traditional horse-drawn coaches, and the structure consisted mainly of wood. The expert handwork of craftsmen therefore was needed and most appreciated.

Within a few years, Jacques Saoutchik

established himself and his small company in this young trade by attractive designs, meticulous work and high quality. In 1909 he built, among others, a fine, traditional coupé de ville on the chassis of a Clement-Bayard. Three years later he advertised his work with the picture of an up-to-date cabriolet for a certain Monsieur de Anchoréna, who belonged to the upper class of the Parisian society. In 1913 one of the silk-smooth Rolls-Royce Silver Ghost chassis obtained a sporty Torpedo body by Saoutchik. This fine car of the Colonial type with 4-speed gearbox still exists, now in the long-held possession of a British enthusiast.

During the first World War there was not much activity by the coachbuilders. Nobody had either the time or pleasure—or the money—for luxury cars. The factories were fully occupied producing ammunition, military vehicles and various other war materiel, and many craftsmen were serving in the army.

After the war, the Automobile Salon of Paris 1919 became a cornerstone of automobile history. Many companies launched new models, which mirrored technical progress. Citroen presented, with their 10 CV Type A, the first economical European car built in large quantities. Hispano-Suiza enthused wealthy sportsmen and connoisseurs with their brand-new model H6. Farman, Bellanger, Voisin and other marques offered powerful and expensive luxury cars.

Apparently Jacques Saoutchik had not yet fallen back into regular step. It took a time until his advertisements reappeared in the motoring periodicals of the time. His coachbuilding company at the Rue Jacques-Dulud No. 46 offered as a speciality a new, patented form of the "Transformable," the convertible suitable for all seasons.

For the famous American silent-movie star Mary Pickford, Saoutchik built a stylish coupé de ville on the expensive Delage CO-chassis. In 1923 followed a very sporty torpedo with double-windscreens on a similar chassis. In this period cabriolets, coupés de ville and limousines on various French and foreign chassis were delivered. The speciality of Saoutchik, "La Transformable" was advertised with a folder, printed in color. A newly invented V-shaped windscreen, consisting of two adjustable parts, was used mainly on sports cars and a patent was applied for it.

RISE AND SUCCESS

The most glorious period of Carrosserie Saoutchik began in the middle of the 1920s. The unmistakable style of the master was developed and became more and more apparent. Whereas the town-cars followed the classical and often stern lines and balanced shapes of tradition, some liberties were taken with the sporty torpedos and touring cars. A French publication of 1926 hailed Saoutchik as one of the greatest coachbuilders of Paris, renown for modern design, large stocks and selection of first-class raw materials, such as wood, leather, cloths, fittings; top craftsmen and highly efficient, spacious workshops.

Typical examples of Saoutchik bodies of the period are a Sedanca de Ville on the powerful chassis of the Hispano-

Fig. 1

Fig. 2

Carrosserie de tourisme sur "MERCÉDÈS

Saoutchik's 1908 sales folder featured this Mercedes tourer, open and closed.

Suiza H6C, the Berline sportive on a Delage six-cylinder DM chassis and the first cabriolet de ville on the supercharged Mercedes-Benz model K.

Mercedes-Benz. The majority was shipped to the United States, where the individualistic bodies by Saoutchik, with their chrome- or nickel-plated decorations and rims of the mudguards, found much appreciation and customers. Often the costly and exclusive Grebel headlamps and movable search-lights were mounted. Even if a few other well-known foreign coachbuilders occasionally made bodies for the expensive Mercedes-Benz cars with the howling supercharger, Saoutchik was by far the most successful with the sophisticated clientele. Highly innovative, he always offered new materials and solutions for the beautiful bodies, which were taken up enthusiastically by the rich, the elegant and the flamboyant of the "Roaring Twenties."

At the end of 1928 a Mercedes-Benz K chassis, with a top speed of about 100 mph, obtained a ravishingly beautiful 4-seater torpedo transformable body with the engine hood and wheel covers made of polished aluminium and with an upholstery and interior of true lizzard skin. Another work by the "Maître de la carrosserie haut luxe" as Saoutchik was admiringly named by the periodical of the trade, Auto-Carrosserie, was the Minerva 32 CV transformable "Empire." It was ordered for the Duchesse de Talleyrand, who not only wanted an outstandingly elegant town-car, but was a great lover of the Napoleonic Empire style. (One of her ancestors, de Talleyrand, was French foreign minister from 1787 till 1807.) Therefore all the gold-plated interior fittings, the upholstery and linings were artfully decorated in Empire patterns. Externally the car had a new moulding extending from the

Thereafter Saoutchik built a whole range of cabriolets, torpedo transformable and town-cars on the mighty chassis model K, S and later SS from

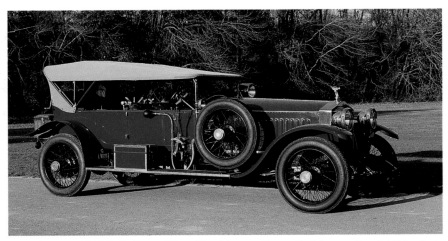

From the top: 1913 Rolls-Royce Silver Ghost tourer, the earliest known Saoutchik-bodied car extant; 1914 Charron 15hp coupé de ville; 1914 Rolls-Royce Silver Ghost torpedo.

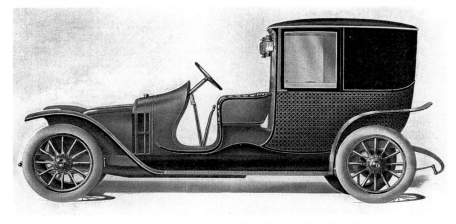

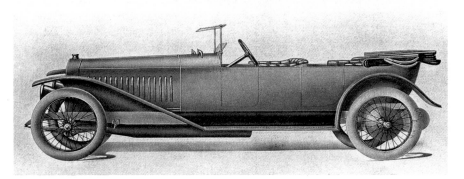

pillars of the windscreen in a handsome curve to the bottom of the engine hood.

It was quite natural that the exquisite creations of Saoutchik won prizes and awards with a nice consistency at the Concours d'Elégance. These were the events which were visited and celebrated by the wealthy society of ladies and gentlemen looking for amusement, recognition and publicity. At the beauty contest of 1929 in Paris, the Minerva 32 CV "Empire" and an exclusive Farman both with Saoutchik bodies were awarded the "Grand Prix d'honneur." In the group of closed cars a Ballot coupé de ville and a Hispano-Suiza faux-cabriolet were in the top range. In Juan les Pins, the fashionable resort on the Mediterrean, Madame del Valle with her Hispano-Suiza cabriolet won the Grand Prix of all classes.

A fine Delage D8 with Saoutchik coupé-limousine body participated in the beauty contest Parc des Princes of Paris and was then offered as a gift to the Negus, the ruler of Abyssinia. In his article in Motor Trend (12/1953), Ernest E. Reshovsky tells us about a telegraphic order in the 1920s for three cars by the King of Siam—one for opera, one for touring and one for his wife. A few months later Saoutchik delivered one Rolls-Royce town car, one Mercedes tourer and one Hispano-Suiza coupé-chauffeur for the royal garages at a reported cost of $60,000. Whenever the French government or industrial empires wanted to express their gratitude or appreciation to foreign heads of state, they often relied on the high prestige and excellent taste of Jacques Saoutchik. Over the years, the kings of Siam (Thailand), Cambodia, Egypt,

Norway and Saudi Arabia were driven in Saoutchik-bodied luxury cars. So was the Shah of Persia.

For the 1929 Paris Salon, Saoutchik had prepared two luxurious cars. The roomy coupé transformable in black had a top which could be completely stored away. Typically, the moulding was made of highly polished aluminum, which started at the engine-hood and dropped in an elegant swing conforming to the raked windscreen to the sill. A novelty was the cover of the upholstery that consisted of narrow plait black leather-stripes. Every 2 inches there was an interruption by a red stripe. The Mercedes-Benz sports torpedo also had an interior made of black-and-red plait leather stripes, which corresponded with the high glossy lacquer of the body.

The American designer Howard "Dutch" Darrin, who together with his partner Thomas L. Hibbard ran a flourishing coachbuilding company in Paris, was an admirer of Saoutchik. "He was a real craftsman, definitely a man with his own ideas," he said. It is interesting to note that Saoutchik's order books are said to have been very discreet, not mentioning names or addresses or the agreed upon prices. They contained only the make and model as well as the chassis number and initials. Compared to big companies, production was always limited and never exceeded two car bodies per week.

Quality was the key word, and the full satisfaction of the customer the paramount goal. Prices were high. If a client asked about them on his first visit of the exhibition stand or show-room, it was likely that he had picked the wrong address. Saoutchik, never-

Above: 1928 Minerva AK convertible (owner: Raymond A. Katzell)
Above right: 1932 Bucciali TAV12 Berline with Voisin sleeve-valve V12 engine
Right: Full-page advertisement for the Rolls-Royce Silver Ghost in Omnia 10/1924

theless, was considered to be quite greedy regarding wages. His employees were required to work to perfection for ten hours on six days of the week. It was a bit like the great chefs-de-cuisine in first-class restaurants. Whoever was allowed to work there was privileged and salary was not considered an aspect of importance.

THE SUMMIT OF APPRECIATION

In the next year, 1930, Jacques Saoutchik reached the zenith of his career. The Hispano-Suiza, Minerva, Mercedes-Benz and Delage were now supplemented by the legendary Duesenbergs, the incredible front-wheel-drive Bucciali and at least one of the famous Maybach "Zeppelin" cars. Promptly, Madame Lebaudy-Sudreau, with her great Duesenberg cabriolet de ville, won the first prize at the June 1930 Concours d'Elégance of Paris. The impressive car was lacquered in a bright colour, with dark, contrasting wings with typical chrome-plated rims and equally polished wheel covers. At the back there was a spacious trunk and two spare wheels.

At the 1930 Paris Salon, the avant-garde Bucciali TAV 30 created much exitement. Compared to conventional luxury cars it was a highly advanced motorcar. The front-wheel-drive permitted a much lower construction and bodyline which was dramatically emphazised by the huge wheels, the low windscreen and the low position of the Grebel headlamps.

With the world-wide economic crisis of the 1930s, many automobile factories ran into financial troubles and the market for expensive, coach-built luxury vehicles began to falter. Saoutchik added more conventional and less expensive chassis from makes such as Lorraine-Dietrich, Delahaye, Georges Irat and Renault to his line. Nevertheless, at least a part of the discriminating clientele kept ordering from the most famous and successful coach-builders even in difficult times. For a few of Saoutchik's customers still only the very best was just good enough. On the new, impressive Hispano-Suiza J12 with its 12-cylinder engine, Saoutchik demonstrated his full mastership with thrilling coupés and cabriolets. One of the better known is the pale-blue two-seater convertible with the 11.3-liter

1947/48 Talbot-Lago T.26 Grand Sport, located at the Rosso-Bianco Museum

1937 Hispano-Suiza K6 coupé de ville

engine owned for many years by the British collector Peter Hampton (see Automobile Quarterly Vol. 16 No. 2). Also the slightly less powerful and less costly model K6 of the famous airplane engine company, which obtained very attractive and carefully finished Saoutchik bodies.

In place of the supercharged Mercedes-Benz, which had by now dropped from the range, Saoutchik turned to Bentley chassis. This make, under the leadership of Rolls-Royce, had mutated to "the silent sports car." New offerings were the convertibles on American chassis from Packard, Graham and others. Again several awards and prizes were won at the Concours d'Elégance.

Since 1932, it was no longer permitted that the fashionably dressed, beautiful women drive the cars in these contests themselves. In '32, Mademoiselle Cardenas, the daughter of a diplomat from South America, had lost control of

her huge Hispano-Suiza H6C. She ran into the thick row of spectators and injured several people. So the smart young ladies could now only present parked cars to the jury for judgment of the ensemble.

A French sportsman, meanwhile, was very impressed by the extravagant new Atlantic coupé design by Jean Bugatti. He requested Saoutchik in 1937 to build a similar body on the fast Bugatti Grand Prix Type 51 chassis he owned. The result was a one of a kind super sports coupé, which due to the shorter wheelbase was not as pleasing as the original.

By 1938, the company's address changed to the Boulevard des Sablons No. 3 in Neuilly. As a novelty, it presented a sliding door, which was fitted with a rod-construction and opened toward the rear and parallel to the car body. Several coupés and cabriolets were thus equipped, among them a Renault for General König, but a true breakthrough

of the idea did not materialize. For the 1939 Paris Salon, Saoutchik prepared a beautiful convertible body on the chassis of a Delage D8-120 with the characteristic external exhaust tubes. Due to the outbreak of World War II, the Salon had to be canceled and later the Delage served as the personal vehicle of General Charles De Gaulle.

When the war ended, the world had changed irrevocably and so had the market for exclusive coachbuilt cars made by the top companies of Paris. At the beginning there was a severe shortage of high-quality material such as leather or special tissues for the upholstery, canvas for the tops, accessories and fittings and even brass, aluminium and sheet-metal. Prestigious marques such as Hispano-Suiza, Isotta-Fraschini, Bugatti and others tried to re-start their activities in the field of automobile production but failed. In France there remained still a handful of traditional manufacturers

of fast touring and sports cars, but this market became increasingly difficult. The chassis of Delage, Delahaye, Talbot-Lago and Hotchkiss were nearly the same they had offered before the war. They again received coachbuilt coupé and convertible bodies, but the demand remained limited and a fresh impetus was not in sight.

Saoutchik was asked in 1946 by the king of the French apéritif makers, Dubonnet, to coachbuild the highly streamlined body of the "Xenia" coupé that he had designed on a pre-war Hispano-Suiza chassis. One year later Saoutchik, who was now associated with Fernandez, changed back the address to the old place at Rue Jacques-Dulud No. 46. Fernandez, also together with the American Darrin, had been active in the 1930s as one of the more fashionable coachbuilders. They specialized in expensive luxury cars, had a good reputation and made among others the bodies for eight Duesenbergs. Alas, the con-

nection was not durable or successful.

In automobile manufacturing, modernization progressed at a very fast pace. Car bodies were built in the factories themselves and in large series. The French taxation system was extremely heavy on the big-capacity engines of luxury cars, favoring small cars for the average citizen. The luxury car prices, when compared to the lower-priced imported cars from England and the United States further curtailed demand and did not promise a rapid recovery.

Saoutchik, who up until 1939 had been committed to rather restrained, traditional forms and a well-balanced style, now began to increasingly engage himself in the creation of the new French fashion of flamboyant car-bodies. The chassis of the French upper-class marques, which became rapidly technically obsolete, received heavy, more and more elaborate bodies made in the classical method with wooden frames. The early post-war models with their long sweeping fenders still had mostly an individual, sensual elegance. Soon, however, the baroque shapes became increasingly bombastic. The unnecessary embellishments and ornaments, often with plenty of chrome-plating, were exaggerated and obtrusive. Some critics—not without reason—called some of these creations grotesque monsters. The complete enclosure of the rear section, and even the front-wheel fenders with spats, made the long convertibles with small tail fins on Talbot and Delahaye chassis of 1947 very bulbous and heavy-looking.

Delahaye T.175 1949 coupé de ville

Soon Saoutchik, just as Figoni & Falaschi and others, reverted to more conventional designs again. In 1948, a Rolls-Royce Silver Wraith with a very peculiar sedanca body won the Grand Prix d'Honneur at the Concours d'Elégance of Monte Carlo. It was the property of John Gaul.

Perhaps one of the best post-war efforts, the strikingly elegant convertible on a Delahaye Type 135 chassis of 1949, was at the beginning of a life-long affair between this marque and the Temperli brothers of Switzerland. Robert Temperli was 16 years old when he bought the car in 1963 at a price of about $70 with his pocket-money savings. Everybody thought him a bit crazy, as he did not have a driver's

This '29 Mercedes-Benz 680 S Torpédo transformable was part of the famous Holterbosch Collection in Long Island from 1970 until 1996. Only seven cars are known to have been bodied by Saoutchik on the Type 680 S chassis, of which only 138 were built. It was powered by a six-cylinder OHC engine with Roots supercharger, producing 225 hp when the supercharger was engaged, and capable of just more than 100 mph. The car was originally owned by Robert Lee Slaughter Jr.

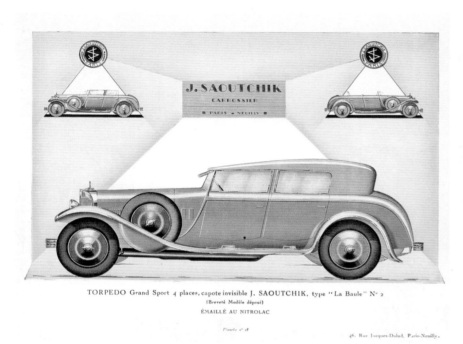

TORPEDO Grand Sport 4 places, capote invisible J. SAOUTCHIK, type "La Baule" N° 2
(Breveté Modèle déposé)
ÉMAILLÉ AU NITROLAC

Planche n° 18   46, Rue Jacques-Dulud, Paris-Neuilly.

The Mercedes-Benz K Torpedo Grand Sport "La Baule" as advertised in the Prestige Sales Catalogue, circa. 1928-1929.

**Above: 1938 Jaguar SS100 roadster, said to be made by Saoutchik.
Below: 1948 Cadillac Series 62**

license and couldn't get one until his 18th birthday. It took him and his brother, Oscar, about 20 years to completely restore the beauty which is now sharing the stable with several other Delahayes (see *Automobile Quarterly* Vol. 39 No. 2, p. 98).

The French fashion obviously was in competition with the creations of the Italian coach-building companies. Apart from some exceptions, where the transalpine masters also did have some trouble with the modern slab-sided bodies, they usually were on the winning side. The neat lines, the mastering of restrained, modern shapes and lack of exaggerated ornaments spoke for itself. In addition, the Italians had advanced and

powerful chassis available, which together with modern light body constructions with steel tubes and aluminum, resulted in superb road performance.

In Neuilly, Saoutchik concentrated his efforts on building a limited number of cabriolets and coupés, some of them now made with light-alloy, on the chassis of Talbot-Lago, Salmson and Delahaye. Occasionally, they also put the bodies on a Cadillac chassis. A full page advertisement in 1950 with coupé and convertible drawings of the Veritas Meteor (which was based on the successful pre-war BMW 327/28) shows the efforts Saoutchik undertook to keep the company afloat. Unfortunately, the small German manufacturer ran out of

funds and no co-operation resulted. In these years, the balance sheet of Saoutchik was probably showing figures in bright red. Some of his extravagant creations found acclaim and attention at the Paris Salon, but they

could not turn the tide. At the Paris Salons, the French coachbuilding companies had their stands at the entrance to the Grand Palais. Saoutchik with No.3 was in the very center. In 1949, a beautiful two-seater convertible on the

1950 Talbot-Lago T.26 GS coupé

1953 Pegaso Z102 convertible

Talbot-Lago Grand Sport, the fastest and most powerful sports car of the time, was a queen of the show.

In 1950 Saoutchik was asked to create a special prestige car for the government of France. The big Talbot-Lago with long chassis obtained an elegant and impressive cabriolet-de-ville body with a center-bar allowing the French president to stand upright in the car on parades. The car was fitted with an electrically operated roof and windows. The interior was finished in pale-blue leather. This was not the first presidental car supplied by Saoutchik. Already in 1929 President Doumergue was travelling in a huge Renault 40 CV landaulet built at Neuilly.

In 1952, the son of Jacques, Pierre Saoutchik (1916-1984), took over the rather ungrateful task of managing the company. At the Paris Salon, a big, dark coupé on a 20-year old Bugatti Type 50 chassis was shown. It competed in the Concours d'Elégance d'Enghien and was honoured by the cup awarded by the association of French coachbuilders.

For the Royal Court of Saudi Arabia, where the spectacular cars apparently were most appreciated, several huge convertibles and limousines were finished. Often the fittings and emblems were gold-plated and the cars had the latest available extras. As King Ibn Saud was partly paralyzed, a special electrically operated swing-out seat was provided. Some cars had refrigerators, hot and cold water, and two-way radio equipment

fitted. The big Cadillac eight-seater convertible on an ambulance chassis was over 22 feet long and contained a half-mile of electric wiring. It is reported to have needed 10,000 working hours to complete.

At the same time, Pegaso, the Spanish truck manufacturers, who also surprisingly offered a modern high-performance sports car, placed an order for the bodies. These Pegaso berlinettas, coupés and convertibles give proof of Saoutchik's endeavours to underline the sporty character of the chassis. He returned to more austere style, reduced weight and obtained better performance. A total of 25 berlinettas and coupés, as well as 12 convertibles were made on this potent and interesting Spanish chassis.

Saoutchik bitterly complained about the lack of support by the French government and the indifference shown by the national car manufacturers. Some studies and prototypes were made for the British Austin, Hillman and Humber. Paul Bracq began his design

career with Saoutchik at this time and was responsible for some attractive proposals of Pegaso bodies. But it was too late already. Bracq moved to Mercedes-Benz and later became chief of the design department with BMW.

In 1955 the irrevocable end came for Carrosserie Saoutchik, who like so many other coachbuilders in France, was unable to recover from the war. Pierre Saoutchik had to depose the balance. His father and founder of the company, which in the 1920s and 1930s proudly counted among its customers the top people of nobility, politics and economy, the stars of theaters, movies and sport, died only two years later.

As an emigrant from troubled and violent Russia, and very humble beginnings in Paris, Jacques Saoutchik had worked his way up to high respect and a certain wealth. In his last years he had to witness the bitter fate of how everything broke down again. **AO**

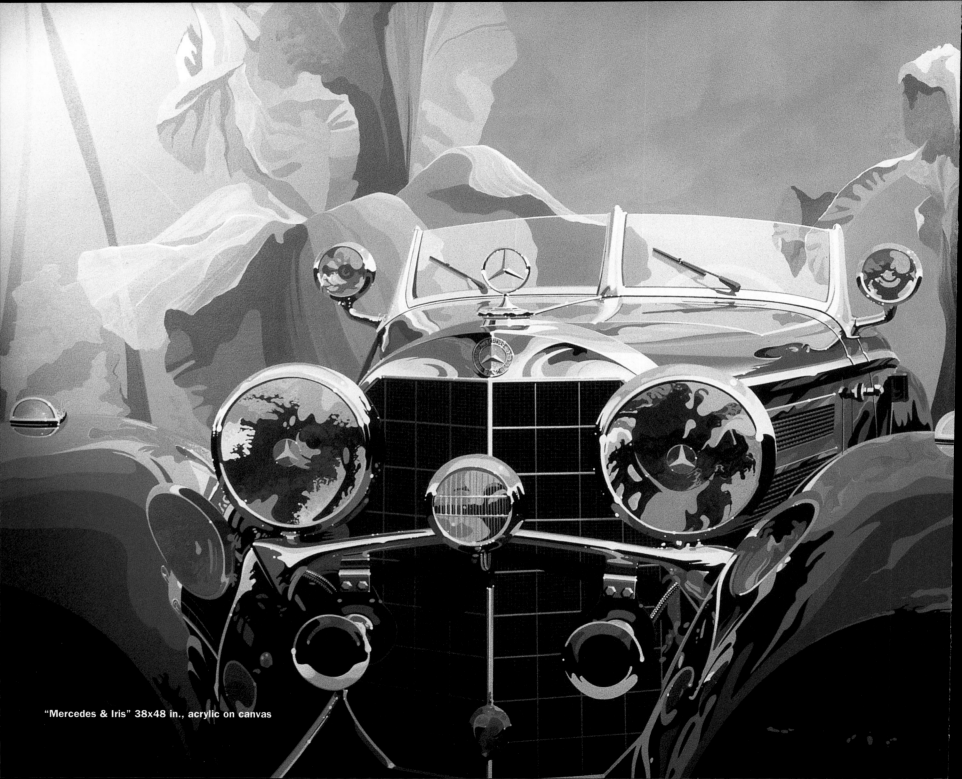

"Mercedes & Iris" 38x48 in., acrylic on canvas

On the Surface
Automotive Art by
TOM HALE

I n one's work, utopia is found when you love what you do. It's even better when you love to live what you do. Such is the case with Tom Hale, a 30-year painting veteran who chucked the well-paid security of a coveted car designer's job for paintbrush and canvas; the same Tom Hale who left an even earlier Big Three-designer gig for a six-month, 25,000-mile road trip, living in a Volkswagen camper.

Try as he might during that freedom-seeking journey in the late hippie era, he couldn't get the notion of car styling out of his mind. "I found myself looking at car magazines, of all things. I couldn't quite stay away from it." Hale found that this fact wasn't necessarily a detriment, that he could combine his love for art and passion for cars to fulfill his destiny in truly unique, painted expression. But it took 17 years after returning to Detroit for that destiny to fully bloom.

BY TRACY POWELL

Part of the reason behind Hale's lingering looks at automobiles is how he spent time, as a boy, with his father, a Chrysler sales rep. The younger Hale traveled with his father from dealership to dealership in the Michigan-Indiana-Ohio region. To kill time while his father conducted business, the younger Hale often sat in showroom cars.

"Back in the early 50s, Chrysler had all those wonderful show cars," says Hale. "Occasionally the dealer would have a show car to promote traffic. The more I sat in these cars, the more intrigued I became with automobiles and design."

So, when people asked him what he wanted to be when he grew up, his answer was always "car designer." Cars and their shapes were so often on Hale's mind, in fact, that he spent more time drawing during class than listening—his high school academic record suffered as a result. But he did graduate, and immediately entered the U.S. Navy, where he was stationed on a destroyer for two years.

"I was fortunate in that I had an office that I was in charge of on the ship, so at the end of the workday I could close the door and sit there and draw cars," says Hale. "At that time I was preparing a portfolio for the Art Center College in California to become a designer. I had to try a couple of times—at first they rejected me and told me I had no potential and knew nothing about color or drawing. It was devastating. My whole life was focused on that moment when I got the letter from the Art Center. Of course, my high school record was pretty weak. Everything I always wanted to be was suddenly dashed—they're telling me I had no potential."

Hale took the school's advice of resubmitting a new portfolio in six months, and was admitted in 1963 on a probationary basis due to his poor high school marks. After the rocky start, barely able to afford to attend, Hale was awarded a scholarship in his third semester, lasting until he graduated … with honors. Hale's talent didn't go unnoticed outside academia—Chuck Jordan visited the campus and offered Hale a job at GM Styling in 1966. Hale and his wife Micki then moved back to Detroit, where he worked for two years.

"Because I had been brought up on Chrysler, I was waiting for the opportunity to go over to Chrysler," says Hale. "Finally an opening came up. I worked at Chrysler for a year and got frustrated with the business … it wasn't quite what I thought or hoped it would be."

Seeking creative freedom, the Hales then took the trip in their VW camper, which turned out to be "one of the high points of our lives." Then the couple returned to Detroit, where Hale worked on American Motors' design team under Dick Teague. Although Ford had made Hale an offer, working at American Motors at the time of the AMX offered Hale an exciting opportunity.

"You couldn't hide there," explains Hale. "They had to use you, and I wanted them to use me. I admired the company—it was a gutsy little company. It turned out to be a pretty significant time in my life."

But not significant in terms of moving up the corporate ladder; in fact, the opposite was true. He became frustrated with lack of creative endeavor, or at least at a level he needed.

"This was actually the reason I began painting—I was just so frustrated, and I had a lot of creative energy with no place to dispense it at work. I started painting on my lunch hour. It was ironic—here I was designing future automobiles and I was painting rusty old trucks, broken down barns and buildings."

Pacifying his deep creative needs in

Above: "Imperial & Tulip Leaves" 20x30 in., poster available. Opposite: "Talbo Lago" 38x48 in,, acrylic on canvas.

Vital elements breath life into Hale's poster work, completed for the 1995 Meadowbrook Concours. Hale sought to make Count Trossi's majestic Mercedes, now owned by Ralph Lauren, an approachable object, even while idling in fantastical surroundings.

the early 1970s by painting landscapes, buildings and other scenes, Hale was taken aback when his wife suggested he try painting cars. Passing the idea off, thinking no one would buy artwork with cars involved, he reconsidered the notion after a man asked him to paint his Rolls-Royce.

"That started it," says Hale. "I never once thought about having a career as an artist. But I enjoyed it, and I could do it for me without answering to anybody. It took on a life of its own, and pretty soon people were interested in buying some of my paintings. Before you know it, I'm starting to do some art shows, entering some competitions and winning an award once in a while. I sort of walked in the back door and started another career."

Hale left American Motors in 1985 "and I haven't looked back."

Ten years ago, a short conversation with his wife resulted in discovering a new concept, which Hale has used ever since to differentiate his paintings.

"One day Micki asked me why I put a tulip on the side of the hood of a car I'd painted. I told her it wasn't a tulip, it was just a red shape, but she said it looked like a tulip," says Hale. "Then I started thinking of how a soft, sensuous flower looked combined with an automobile."

That prompted Hale, in 1992, to incorporate floral images with automobiles. For him, he's getting the best of two worlds in his paintings now: beauty in nature and in man-made design.

"I find that flowers are some of the most beautiful things in nature—they're soft, they're sensuous, they have wonderful and brilliant colors," says Hale. "And automobiles are the most incredible things that man has produced. On top of being reliable and functional, they're made to be beautiful in terms of the finishes, styling and detail. I feel flowers and cars complement each other perfectly in a painting."

Using flowers is a device that allows Hale to reflect various shapes and unusual colors on top of the car, something often unattainable. Consider that objects normally reflected on tops of automobiles—such as sky tone, a building or tree—are extremely limited in type, shape and color.

"My painting of cars has never been formula," says Hale. "When I went to Art Center, they taught you a formula on how to render a car. Many artists are satisfied with using that basic formula. I didn't ever want to do that; I wanted all of my lighting, all of my rendering, to be more creative and a lot freer."

Using flora is also an extension of Hale's artistic approach, which tends toward organic surrealism. This organic approach is vivid in paintings like "Meadowbrook," a poster Hale completed for the 1995 Meadowbrook concours. Using an enormous flower, the beautiful grounds and Count Trossi's Mercedes owned by Ralph Lauren, Hale managed to capture what many attendees experience at such events.

"You take the average person that comes to a concours, like Meadowbrook," says Hale, "and they see a couple hundred of the most incredible cars in the world, they see a 110-room mansion that's bigger than life, beyond anything

Above: A Lincoln Zephyr is caught in Hale's marvelously different light in "Lincoln & Calla" 49x65x2 in., acrylic on canvas.

Right: "Chrysler Airflow" 30x40 in., acrylic on board; the original is available.

Below: "Delahaye" 30x40 in., acrylic on board; the original is available.

Passion plays out in "Mercedes 540K" 36x48 in., acrylic on canvas.

Sensuality meets the canvas, with flowing vertical contours in "Jaguar XKE" (left) 36x48 in., acrylic artwork, and stunning reflection in "Packard and Rose" (right) 42x74 in., acrylic on canvas. These elements are almost always present as Hale marries the beauty of both flower and automobile.

they can imagine, they see these luxurious rolling grounds. For the average guy on the street, the total scene is surreal—nobody can live in a 110-room mansion; nobody can afford this $5-million car. And yet, the mansion's real and the car's real. What I tried to do is get the element of fantasy that some of these people might see when they come to a concours event."

In the organic sense, pointed note is taken of Hale's ability to bring the Mercedes to life with elements of heat around the exhaust pipes, as well as a trickle of exhaust rising in the air. A giant flower beside the car reflects on the car's deck to create another element of life amidst grand surroundings, the central element of which is an incredible car. It's the play on the car's surface that, for Hale, captures the fantastical environment.

"I know a lot of people are fascinated with the historical significance of the car; maybe its racing history, the particular engineering of the car," says Hale. "But in my case all my fascination is about the surface of the automobile. I imagine these surfaces as my canvases, creating brilliant, reflective colors, particularly off chrome.

"I like the forms I'm dealing with that create flowing, abstract patterns on the sculptured countours. My interest lies in capturing this excitement and conveying it to the viewer."

Hale can be as excited about the detail off an old Plymouth as he can off an old Packard.

"If it gives me an opportunity to reflect and do something on it that I think is exciting in terms of patterns and composition, it doesn't matter what

Left: "Mercedes 300SL" 30x40 in., acrylic on board.
Above: "Duesenberg & Rose" 44x66 in., acrylic on canvas.
Opposite: Award-winning "Chrome" 30x40 in., acrylic on watercolor board.

tablishing some sort of credibility for this kind of art in the art world. The credibility we get is minimal. It forces me to work even harder."

One approach Hale takes to offset this widely held attitude is showing his work at non-automotive art shows. As early as 1980, before leaving American Motors, Hale accomplished a victory toward this cause by showing "Chrome" and subsequently winning the American Watercolor Society's (AWS) Gold Medal of Honor—the only automotive work to have done so in the society's 134-year history.

"Even to this day,

type of car it is. I'm always looking and discovering things. I may look at the same car at 15 or 20 different shows and all the sudden, one day it really hits me."

But Hale's artistic convictions also go beneath the surface—of the art community's perception of automotive work, that is. He and other automotive artists continue to hold up a banner that pronounces the validity of portraying the automobile in works of art, equal to what is found in many art galleries according to Hale.

"For 30 years I've struggled with es-

all of us that do automotive art run into a brick wall when it comes to galleries and curators and museums because they write it off as a commercial form of art," notes Hale. "Regardless of how good it is and how much art content it has, all they see is the automobile; they can't see beyond that. It's really frustrating. When I was awarded the gold medal in the conservative, prestigious AWS with the 1932 Duesenberg painting, it was thrilling. I felt it was a huge step forward in getting some acceptance for the subject of the automobile in the art field." **AQ**

FRAN —
YOU ARE WONDERFUL
LOVE.
Tom

TOM HALE

ROUTE 66: The Mother Road

Main Street of the Nation

If the heart of America's early 20th Century industrial prosperity was the automobile, then the main artery was Route 66, the highway that allowed Americans to fulfill their unique passion for conquering its western frontier, propigated long-distance travel that was available to the masses, and birthed a treasure of legends, myths and an endless heritage.

BY JULIE FENSTER

The frontier was supposed to be closed. A young historian named Frederick Jackson Turner had given the nation a jolt by making that pronouncement in 1893. With the American West not only explored, but fully surveyed and mostly settled, the population "is now thrown back upon itself," Turner wrote. His theory was no mere academic musing. It rocked the whole country, because, as it acknowledged, part of being American was having that frontier always in mind and knowing exactly what it meant: freedom of the most individual kind.

Frederick Turner went on to a distinguished career, leaving the rest of the nation with an identity crisis to muddle through. The frontier was closed and so was all that went with it. "This perennial rebirth, this fluidity of American life," Turner had said, "this

expansion westward with its new opportunities, its continuous touch with the simplicity of primitive society, furnish the forces dominating American character."

For decades afterward, America lived with the claustrophobia that was all that remained to furnish the force of its character. Then in 1926, one of the earliest national highways opened, leading from Chicago through the Southwest to Los Angeles. It was

christened Route 66. The frontier was open again.

MORE THAN A HIGHWAY

Route 66 was everything that Turner had said a frontier should be—in reality and in the minds of Americans prone to daydreaming. At every level it offered a rebirth and

fluidity, new opportunities by the mile and expansion westward to a goldfield called Southern California. As to primitive society, Route 66 offered it in a panorama of the Wild West, or what was left of it. Just as intriguing, though, was the primitive society that Route 66 generated on its

Frederick Turner Jackson

A scenic stretch of Route 66 near Oatman, Arizona, and the Colorado River. Despite the number of travelers and sightseers over its years of its existence, the sections of road still used have been maintained and are in remarkably good condition.

52

own: the garish drive-ins and over-anxious attractions beckoning to the millions who drove by.

From 1926 to 1977, when the old route was replaced in the national highway system, they came by the car-full, tourists on a spree, Oakies fleeing tapped-out farms, truck drivers, landlocked beach bums determined to touch the Pacific Ocean and people moving out West for good. Of course, Route 66 wasn't a one-way road. It also aimed east, yet no one ever described it as a road from Los Angeles to Chicago. The record of Californians yearning to see Lake Michigan is remarkably scant. Eastward migration to Missouri was never much of a trend. Route 66 was indeed a beacon pointing west, built for those with a natural inclination to follow the Sun.

That inclination and the way that Route 66 brought three generations of Americans closer to the Sun entered into modern folklore. Writers spotted that fact early and used Route 66, its hope and pathos, in their work. John Steinbeck labeled it "the Mother Road" when describing the Joad family following it west from Oklahoma in "The Grapes of Wrath" (1939).

The "Mother" was what it meant to people traveling without maps: only two Sixes they trusted to bring them to a new life in California. Robert Sherwood set his 1934 play, "The Petrified Forest", in a filling station and BBQ along Route 66, where the main character is "gipsying." As he explained: "I had a vague idea that I'd like to see the Pacific Ocean, and perhaps drown in it." More than words, though, it was a beat that captured

Route 66 in pop culture: the impatient, staccato beat of the song made famous by Nat King Cole. "Get Your Kicks on Route 66," it insisted, doing little more with the lyrics than naming the towns along the way.

Starting in Chicago, originally at the corner of Jackson Boulevard at Michigan Avenue, Route 66 led southwest through Illinois, past Abraham Lincoln's hometown of Springfield to the easterner's first big 66 thrill: the Chain of Rocks Bridge crossing the Mississippi River at St. Louis. After that, the route traced a string of small towns across Missouri—towns like Cuba, Hazel Green and Avilla, before nipping into Kansas just to clip a dozen or so miles off the corner.

Through those first few states, Route 66 fell on a fairly steep southwestern swing, but it straightened out gently in Oklahoma, catching the big cities of Tulsa and Oklahoma City along with a good look at farmland in every direction. Heading almost due west the rest of the way, the route missed the Oklahoma panhandle but made a straight shot through the Texas one, loping along through ranch towns like Shamrock and Amarillo.

Route 66 changed every place it touched, but had the biggest effect on New Mexico and Arizona. As of 1926, when the new highway was mapped out, they were the newest states in the union, having been granted statehood only 14 years before. Newness was not the appeal, however. It was the refreshing antiquity of the former territories that

ROUTE 66

If you ever plan to motor west;
travel my way, take the highway that's the best.
Get your kicks on Route Sixty-Six!

It winds from Chicago to L.A.,
more than two thousand miles all the way.
Get your kicks on Route Sixty-Six!

Now you go thru Saint Looey Joplin, Missouri
and Oklahoma City is mighty pretty.
You'll see Amarillo, Gallup, New Mexico;
Flagstaff, Arizona; don't forget Winona,
Kingman, Barstow, San Bernardino.

Won't you get hip to this timely tip:
When you make that California trip.
Get your kicks on Route Sixty-Six!
Get your kicks on Route Sixty-Six!

Words & music by Bobby Troup; Renewed Copyright 1973, Londontown Music

intrigued motorists from the east. Attractions such as the Rocky Mountains, the Petrified Forest, gigantic saguaro cactus, and the Joshua Tree Forest set a backdrop, at least until the roadside grew into an attraction

Albuquerque and Gallup in New Mexico were longtime trading posts that concentrated new efforts on commerce with the coming of Route 66. Flagstaff and Kingman, both used as gateways to the Grand Canyon and other natural attractions, anchored Route 66 in Arizona. The last 200 miles across California were the most daunting of the whole trip, with the Mojave Desert lying like a deadly, slow-

moving snake between Needles on the California-Arizona border and the cool waves of the Pacific. If motorists could still chuckle when they saw that the midway point was a crossroads called Siberia, they were practically home free. But they still had to continue through Barstow, San Bernardino and Pasadena to L.A.'s Santa Monica Boulevard. The road didn't stop moving west until it hit the beach.

From the start, Route 66 built on its own legend: more travelers encouraged more restaurants and diversions, which drew yet more tourists. James E. Cook was a teenager in Flagstaff in the early 1950s. "I'd sit in a booth at the Round

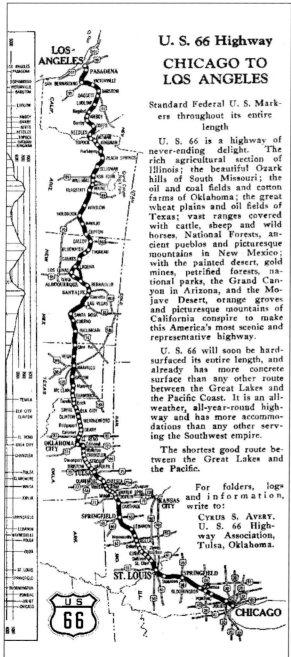

U. S. 66 Highway

CHICAGO TO LOS ANGELES

Standard Federal U. S. Markers throughout its entire length

U. S. 66 is a highway of never-ending delight. The rich agricultural section of Illinois; the beautiful Ozark hills of South Missouri; the oil and coal fields and cotton farms of Oklahoma; the great wheat plains and oil fields of Texas; vast ranges covered with cattle, sheep and wild horses, National Forests, ancient pueblos and picturesque mountains in New Mexico; with the painted desert, gold mines, petrified forests, national parks, the Grand Canyon in Arizona, and the Mojave Desert, orange groves and picturesque mountains of California conspire to make this America's most scenic and representative highway.

U. S. 66 will soon be hard-surfaced its entire length, and already has more concrete surface than any other route between the Great Lakes and the Pacific Coast. It is an all-weather, all-year-round highway and has more accommodations than any other serving the Southwest empire.

The shortest good route between the Great Lakes and the Pacific.

For folders, logs and information, write to:

CYRUS S. AVERY, U. S. 66 Highway Association, Tulsa, Oklahoma.

Cyrus Avery

Up Cafe watching the world pass," Cook recalled of his teenage years in the early 1950s.

The Round Up was at the corner of Leroux Street and Santa Fe Avenue in downtown Flagstaff. Santa Fe, the Main Street in Flagstaff, was also U.S. 66, the Main Street of America. In summer, cars were bumper-to-bumper on the narrow street. Lots of older cars, of course, but also the boxy post-1949 Fords, bullet-nosed Studebakers, Buicks with portholes, Cadillacs with fins. You didn't see many foreign cars then.

Sometimes the cafe was so crowded with travelers that the management didn't appreciate teenagers hanging out, nursing coffee or Cokes, and ogling the tourist girls. For 40 years, Route 66 was the best-known route across the West. But it was neither the first, nor the only route at a time when national routes and the boosters behind them—competed for travelers with as much verve as the train companies.

In 1922, the United States counted approximately 17 million vehicles, most of them used only close to home, except on pristine days in the summer. The majority of rural roads were unpaved. The gentlest mizzle—let alone a downpour—made the driving ugly. To extend the reach and subsequent influence of the automobile, a determined "Good Roads Movement" had been at work in various forms—both public and private—for more than a dozen years.

Its most famous achievement was the Lincoln Highway, conceived largely as a chain of existing roads, well marked and upgraded. Most of these roads existed, at any rate. But some of them didn't. The 1915 "Official Road Guide" noted, for instance, that the Lincoln Highway was passable, at least up to the sand and gravel pathway of a town called Fish Springs, Utah: "If trouble is experienced," the "Road Guide" advised, "build a sagebrush fire. Mr. Thomas will come with a team."

That sort of thing was all right for vacationers looking for a bit of adventure in the middle of the summer, but it wasn't practical for anyone else. Many took the train and so did the nation's cargo. From the Federal government's point of view, the most important of all of the nation's vehicles were the 2 million trucks on American roads. Trucks, after all, were business.

Above: Hair-pin curve of a section of what was once the National Old Trails Highway, and later a part of Route 66, in Arizona. It didn't take long for "filling stations" to spring up at all points along the route.

And after seeing hard service during World War I, these trucks had become tough, long-distance haulers. So if trucks were fit to make interstate trips, then America was ready to pay for interstate highways.

In 1921, the government passed the Federal Highway Act, by far the most ambitious road-building initiative in the United States up to that time. It marked the beginning of what would become the century's greatest public works effort: the national highway system. The law called for the government to share the cost of highways that were to be built, owned and maintained by the individual states. As the situation unraveled, the cars were waiting to get onto improved roads and the government was ready to help pay for them.

By 1923, more than 200 booster clubs had sprung up throughout the country, intent on bringing road mania past their own doors. Without regard for government highway planners, they leapt into their own maps. In general, the boosters followed the Lincoln Highway formula of charting a likely route and then sealing it with an appealing name.

Before Route 66 began to be transformed by sections of wide-laned highways and interstates, the much-traveled highway zipped through downtowns of some very small communities, like Winslow, Arizona (above). Opposite: 1951 Chevy pickup in front of a restored Standard Oil Station in Odell, Illinois,

That done, they boosted it in the press and with people who counted, looking for government money and public interest. Some of the booster groups were little more than real estate cartels, hoping to turn worthless stretches of country lane into boom towns.

The result was a generation of highways with names such as the Victory Highway (Missouri-Utah); the Dixie Overland Highway (Georgia-Texas) and the King of Trails (Missouri-South Dakota). One of the few still known by its original "booster" name is the Pacific Highway (Route 1), which runs the length of the West Coast.

The most important of all were the trans-continental highways. By 1923, the nation counted four of them,

including the Lincoln Highway: the Yellowstone Trail (Boston to Seattle), the National Old Trails Road (Washington to Los Angeles) and the Old Spanish Trail (Jacksonville, Florida to San Diego). They each had their seasons, but none was practical on a year-round basis, due to the extremes of the weather in the northern and very southern parts of the country. Cyrus Avery, an Oklahoman who had risen to national prominence in highway planning, recognized that the best route through the west had yet to be marked. He connected existing roads along a Chicago-to-Los Angeles route that would neither duck as far south as the Dixie Overland Highway, which hugged the Rio Grand River, nor slog through the snows like the more

northerly National Old Trails Road. Looping through the Rockies in northern New Mexico and Arizona, it generally promised motorists straight terrain and clear weather. The route also managed to miss very little of Avery's home state of Oklahoma.

Even if Cy Avery had an ulterior motive in plotting highways through the Southwest, his prejudice was well-timed. In 1925, when he was planning his new route, the United States counted 274,911 miles in its highway system. Less than three-quarters of one percent of those roads were in Arizona (2,014 miles). By any standard, the Southwest was lagging behind in road-building.

As a recognized highway official, Avery managed to

rise above the fray of the booster clubs and, in 1926, his road was duly designated as a national highway. It covered 2,648 miles, only about 800 of it paved. Corny names having given way to officious numbers, the highway was called Route 60 at first. The signs went up, but they didn't remain. After a long struggle with Tennessee, which wanted that number for one of its own highways, Avery suddenly capitulated and took the strangely irresistible "66"

for his road. And 66 remained his road, even after the government took up its keep. In 1927, Avery co-founded his own booster group, the Route 66 Highway Association.

The history of driving has long depended on the progress of three interdependent elements: the highway, the automobile and the driver. That interdependence is too

often overlooked. Automobiles are studied from every angle, yet their development was influenced at every stage by the state of highway conditions, as well as by the training or lack thereof of drivers. In Europe, good roads tended to come first, followed by mass-production cars that would meet their potential. America, as a general trend, built better cars than it had roads on which to drive them. In 1926, when Route 66 was launched, a magazine

suggested that highway motorists plan on traveling about 150 miles per day. By 1938, when the last parcel of the route was finally paved in cement, most cars cruised its long straightaways at 50 mph, and 300 miles in a day was the norm. Unless, of course, the driver gave in and stopped to see some sights—an alligator farm or real Indian village— along the way. Or unless the old truck was loaded up with relatives and other belongings, and couldn't roll along at more than about 30 mph.

In 1939, designer and soothsayer Norman Bel Geddes startled the New York World's Fair by predicting in General Motors' Futurama exhibit that cars would travel at 100 mph someday soon. After World War II, when American cars were capable of touring at nearly that speed, Route 66 became a favorite GT trip for anyone looking to test a powerful car. The marvelously lucid ruling was that where no speed limit was posted, there was no speed limit. And so the two-lane concrete road in the desert was, for some daredevils, a 100-mph highway. It wasn't built for

such speeds, though, nor for the increase in traffic that clogged highways throughout the country in the 1950s and 1960s.

As the Supreme Allied Commander directing troops both during and after World War II, Gen. Dwight Eisenhower had taken an especially good look at

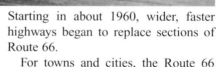

European roads and Germany's fledgling Autobahn system. After his election as President in 1952, he instigated a road construction plan to push road quality up to the standard of vehicle quality—and quantity as well. Under his administration, the Interstate Highway System was launched.

Starting in about 1960, wider, faster highways began to replace sections of Route 66.

For towns and cities, the Route 66 years were a transition between the previous century of train travel and the current era of limited access highways. Both traded freedom for speed. On either a train or a superhighway between exits (or a jet airplane, most of all), a traveler might as well be zooming through a vacuum tube, with no proximity at all to people or places along the way. Architecture is hidden, faces non-existent, animals look like dots and plants are just colors in a field.

But for a few decades in the middle of the 20th Century, the quick way was also the memorable way—the adventurous, eye-catching and enter-

taining way. Highways all over the country paraded right through downtowns: big ones like Philadelphia or Houston, but tiny ones, too. For the traveler, a road like Route 66 was not merely a chance to go somewhere, but a chance to be somewhere and to see it close-up. No wonder nostalgia gathers around the route today.

For a village, the decision to run a national route through town was equivalent to the gods suddenly tossing down a new river. The river was made of cars, but the people inside the cars spelled the same thing as people anywhere: potential. What was the difference between a bustling city of 80,000 and a hamlet of 1,000 with 79,000 people driving through every day? Nothing at all, at least to the businesses that sprang up to capitalize on the hungry, curious, tired and bored. The hell-bent intention to stop the river and snag the travelers led to signs that grew bigger and bigger through the years, architecture that grew crazier and more colorful, food that grew cheaper and faster—and curiosities that grew less and less interesting.

As that roadside circus began to proliferate, America's more thoughtful citizens were outraged. "Once," observed an editorialist in *House & Garden* magazine in the mid-1920s, "travelers along the highways gazed at scenery; now they catch fleeting glimpses of billboards. Once they went leisurely to an inn; now they rush furiously from filling station to filling station. All you find on the modern American highway today are billboards and filling stations. The fine admiration of a tree in autumn foliage is broken by

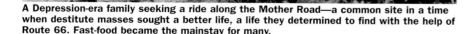

A Depression-era family seeking a ride along the Mother Road—a common site in a time when destitute masses sought a better life, a life they determined to find with the help of Route 66. Fast-food became the mainstay for many.

The newly organized New Mexico Motor Patrol makes a stop along Route 66 in 1933 near Santa Fe. It was believed among motorists that in areas where the speed limit wasn't posted, there was indeed no speed limit. Many tested the theory. Traditionalists found billboards and other aspects of commercialism more troublesome, however, than undeterred speedsters.

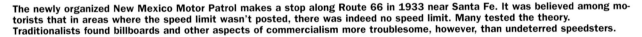

the suggestion to eat hot dogs."

A writer in the Saturday Evening Post in 1932 described the effect of swarming businesses and advertisers on the highways as "obscenic scenery." Certain eastern states, he was glad to report, were already enforcing zoning and enacting laws to restrict billboards. The western states didn't follow suit and so there was nothing to stop the commercial tangle that grew on Route 66. Sprouting robustly whether in a cornfield or a desert, roadside distractions and tourist attractions made Route 66 America's Main Street, all

right, with all that implied for the rest of the country. Beautification was knocked into the gutter.

So was a rural way of life. "There is another phase to the roadside lunch stand and to the roadside gasoline filling station which provides food for serious thought," observed House & Garden. "The men and women and children who tend them were once occupied with country industries. The men farmed, the women had their household work and the children did chores. Today an appreciable part of the time and energy of these people is

devoted to the lunch counter and the gasoline pump ... You wonder, as the farmer's lad dishes up a plate of hot dogs, if he has yet been taught how to plough a straight furrow, if he still churns butter and splits kindling."

That was the scenario on Route 66, as farmers with land abutting the highway often turned to pumping gas, renting cabins or selling gimcracks. It was just plain easier than churning butter or splitting wood— a concept at

the base of all urban civilization, even its outposts. The cars on the national highways brought the city to the country. If highways were like rivers, they had the power to bring new energy, as well as erode old foundations.

"'Course everything you get you must pay for in one way or another," Will Rogers wrote in 1929. "Cars made good roads. Good roads killed small

Many of Route 66's noted oddities like the Wigwam Motel in Holbrook, Arizona, still exist and are still in business.

towns. Small towns was where all our best thinkers come from. So cars haven't been quite as cheap as we think they have." That observation was probably forgotten by the time Route 66 was named for Will Rogers in 1952.

Today, the old battles over the wanton ugliness of commercialism along Route 66 is forgotten, a war long since lost

along thousands of "America's main streets." Once its disgrace, the quick-glance architecture is recognized today as the glory of Route 66: the Fat Boy hamburger stands and Teepee Motels. At least, it is a reminder of a time when such garishness was folk-made—not franchised.

While other national routes had

their share of roadside life, on Route 66 it came to be regarded as high art. "Before Route 66 changes forever take a look at it," advised an editorial in The New Republic in 1956, the year Eisenhower's highway act took effect. "The quick lunch, the filling–stations (each advertising 'ice water' and competing for the

smallest decimal '9' after the gasoline price), the stark line of telegraph poles marching across the continent, the arid prairie coming unfenced to the highway, the wandering dog, the rooster crowing—these things fill the scene."

"Merely putting it down is a

Valentine," the writer added at the end. "Route 66 I love you." He wasn't the only one.

By the end in the early 1970s, Route 66 was still the most fun way to go east or west in the West, but "66" was doomed. The same states that had long boasted of "America's Main Street" betrayed it in favor of those four- and six-lane interstates that speed the pace—and numb the soul. The road that was part of American literature in the 1930s and 1940s is a nostalgic part of the collective memory today. There are state and national clubs devoted to the Mother Road, along with at least a half-dozen books, ranging from scholarly photographic essays and oral histories to cookbooks, volumes devoted to collectibles, and several in-depth guidebooks. Souvenirs are still hot sellers, particularly reproductions of the original road signs. Though the route was officially decommissioned years ago and vast sections have been taken over by weeds, a tour of the old road is still a compelling vacation; as much now as ever.

No other old highway is glamorized the same way. Come to think of it, no other American highways are glamorized at all; we throw them away along with the cars and the paper cups as soon as a better ride comes along. Apparently, Route 66 was different from the very start, a stretch of concrete that could perfect the triumvirate of road, driver and car. AO

The Harrah Collection

The National Automobile Museum
Reno, Nevada

Cars drove Bill Harrah's life from an early age. His passion grew out of a childhood enthusiasm for an invention in its infancy. In the mid- to late-1910s, every time an out-of-town vehicle passed by his childhood home in rural Southern California, a young Harrah ran to the street to commit its automotive features to memory. As a teen, he took jobs where he could drive others' vehicles. Eventually, he amassed more than 1,400 vehicles—one of the world's largest collections. And while he made no provisions for his cherished collection upon his death, the collection's essence lives on in the National Automobile Museum (The Harrah Collection) in Reno, Nevada.

BY KATHY BERRY

63

One of the oldest in the collection, the 1903 Cadillac A Runabout.

ascinated by cars since he was a little boy, Harrah did all he could to be around them. During downtown trips, he memorized hubcap and radiator details. In games to name the most cars, Harrah could list more than even the adults; he knew all the rare models. His father, who must have understood his son's love of cars, allowed Harrah to not only get his driver's license at age 12, but

he also falsified the license application to say that his 12-year-old was actually 14, the legal driving age! This important document gave Harrah the ability to take jobs at area parking lots where he drove a wide variety of other people's cars.

At 15, he acquired his first new car— a 1926 Chevrolet Roadster. "It's the only stock car I ever had," Harrah laughed while sharing his stories with a University of Nevada historian in 1978,

the year he died. Harrah couldn't resist a few modifications to this stock car— he lowered it, changed the wheels and painted them, nickel-plated the headlights and dashboard, and added so many spotlights, running-board lights and road lights that the car sported 26 lights in all. Regardless of day or night, people knew when Harrah approached before they could see him. He had installed 11 horns on it as well.

STARTING HIS COLLECTION

o Harrah, car collecting was a noble pursuit. He believed himself a savior of cars: a missionary spreading the word about this illustrious invention and all of its incarnations.

But his prestigious collection may not have been created if not for a tragic

Bill Harrah stands amidst a handful of his cars in 1968. Clockwise from Harrah: 1933 Weymann-bodied SJ Duesenberg, 1929 Mercedes-Benz SSK, 1915 Dodge Brothers, 1927 Franklin, 1913 Pierce-Arrow, 1900 Packard, 1909 Thomas K 6-70 Flyabout, 1929 Model A Ford, 1932 Marmon V16 and a 1929 Buick.

accident and a later embarrassment. His good friend Johnny Vogel died in a car accident when coming to visit Harrah in Reno during the 1940s. Vogel's mother wanted to give her son's cars to him, but he insisted on paying $2,000 for the supposed 1907 Maxwell and $1,500 for a 1911 Ford Model T Roadster. Harrah hired a mechanic to hop-up and restore the Maxwell and, then took it to the Horseless Carriage Club tour in Southern

California. While at the tour's Ocean-side lunch stop, club member Bud Catlett surveyed Harrah's Maxwell and said, "Is this the right radiator? Is this a 1907? It looks more like a 1911."

Harrah, a bit defensive, didn't like anyone telling him his 1907 could be a 1911 car "because older was better." But once Harrah got home and re-searched the Maxwell, he found "that Catlett was absolutely right and I was as

wrong as could be." The 1907 was actu-ally a 1911 Maxwell AB Runabout. This humbling experience propelled Harrah's determination for restoration authentic-ity and his quest for a complete auto-motive library.

When Harrah saw a car he liked, he bought it. By 1959 his collection had grown to 49 cars—mostly open cars, such as tourings and roadsters. At that time, Harrah decided to get a better

cross section of autos and started look-ing at other body types.

Harrah made his first large purchase in 1961 after giving it 10 full minutes of consideration. Jack Nethercutt (of Merle Norman Cosmetics) called Harrah one day to propose that he buy Nethercutt's 30 classic cars for $150,000—about half of the collection's value at that time. Nethercutt insisted on two stipulations, however: Harrah had to pay cash and

This 1933 Cadillac V16 Fleetwood was custom built for Al Jolson.

Nethercutt had to have the money brought to him in Los Angeles within two days. To Harrah, this deal was more than tempting. Most of Nethercutt's cars were beautifully restored and included four J and SJ Duesenbergs, nine Packards, a duPont Town Car and three Rolls-Royces. After speaking with his financial advisor, Harrah called Nethercutt immediately and closed the deal.

Harrah later acquired other car collections as well, including the Rockefellers' and singer Jimmy Melton's. Harrah especially liked the 1917 Winton Custom House Car he acquired from Melton. Made in the teens, its rear end reminded him of a "train." Harrah paid for it and had the title, but by the time one of his employees went to pick it up, it had been repossessed for a debt

Melton owed. After getting a runaround from authorities, Harrah called his Horseless Carriage Club friend and former Sacramento policeman Catlett (at that time, Catlett also worked for Harrah) and told him, "Go back and if you can steal that damn Winton, steal it! It's our car." Catlett waited until the sheriff's deputy, who was guarding the car, left for dinner. He then drove the sputtering and missing vehicle across the state line.

To find the cars on his wish list, Harrah enlisted the help of local "car lookers." These men—usually friends of the collection—were very car savvy. But Harrah didn't get everything he wanted. Among the cars that got away was

the high-performance 1908 Chadwick. His staff scoured the nation for this rarity, finally locating one on a Minnesota farm. The Chadwick had been sitting out in a field so long that a tree had grown up between the frame. Harrah's men rushed out to the farm to find the car gone and the tree freshly cut down. Only a few days earlier, one of Harrah's rivals, Bill Pollack, had bought the car.

THE COLLECTION GOES PUBLIC

Three different factors played into Harrah's decision to make his private collection public: broadening Reno's tourist appeal and therefore increasing his hotel/casino business, making car history come alive for others as it had for him, and justifying his desire to have his collection under one roof. "What are you going to do with 100 cars?" Harrah had mused. 'Well, gee, I should have a museum; I should have 'em in a building." Prior to the leasing of an ice warehouse in a Reno suburb, Harrah's vehicles had been scattered throughout the area.

Harrah took on the responsibility of accurately portraying the history of the automobile. When Harrah's Automobile Collection opened to the public in 1962, Harrah made it a point to showcase interesting features, car developments and automobiles with historical significance. "You can see pictures in books and the original factory ad, but to actually see the car sitting there is so far ahead of the rest."

Automotive writer Michael Lamm, who regularly spent three to four days in a single visit to Harrah's Automobile Collection, called it "the world's best living reference work on the history of the American automobile." By 1975, the collection included 1,417 automobiles, 13 boats, 12 airplanes, 64 motorcycles, 38 children's cars and 11 assorted vehicles, such as a cable car and a motorized toboggan. All were housed in three warehouses. The roster of cars was impressive

Harrah was a lover of speed, an example being Kurtis race cars ('55 Kurtis above, middle). Below: "Modern Street Scene" is the walkway between Gallery 2 (showcasing cars from 1914-1931), Gallery 3 (cars from 1932-1954) and Gallery 4 (cars from 1954-present, including the museum's race car collection). Meticulous care is administered to each car via the museum's professional restoration facilities (right).

whether it was the row-upon-row of Fords—139 in all, representing most every year from the 1903 A to the 1976 Thunderbird V-8—or his fine Bugatti collection. Visitors then gawked at the 16 Bugattis, among them two of the six existing Bugatti Type 41 Royales and the first Bugatti ever made: the 1908 Type 10 Petit Pur Sang. Ettore Bugatti built this in his home's basement in Cologne, Germany while employed as a chief engineer of Gasmototren-Fabrik Deutz. Harrah's collection also housed 18 Duesenbergs, documenting every year of production from 1922 to 1936, including the 1927 X Sport Touring model, one of 11 built.

Each week, Harrah divied up the time between his cars and his company: he spent 15 hours a week at the collection and 30 hours a week with his hotel-casino. This casino background shaped his philosophy against insuring his automobiles. "We call it self-insurance, which is no insurance, because that's our business—the gamblin' business—and why pay them?"

HARRAH AND HIS RESTORATION SHOP

Harrah mandated that all restorations be historically accurate. Bringing a car back to its factory-shipped condition was a tremendous kick for him. When Harrah's staff com-

pleted a restoration, he said it "really feels like I've done something … if it wasn't for me, it wouldn't ever have been done."

In the '60s, his collection employed 150 people, 75 of whom restored cars. His crew consisted of upholsterers, mechanics, painters, body men, machinists, woodworkers, sandblasters and more. "We never had as many restorers as we'd have liked. I would've liked to have maybe double what we've had in mechanics and in painters and woodworkers, but you can only do so much."

Every car slated for restoration had a manual created specifically for it. These meticulous manuals covered every detail of the automobile such as paint details and samples, correct car items, nickel plating and original manufacturer literature. Restorers regularly enlisted the assistance of the library's researchers for historically accurate information. All cars marked for restoration were

classified in one of eighteen car condition categories. The top rating, "Gold Star," gave Harrah's staff carte blanche to achieve a total, authentic restoration that was agreeable with management, namely Harrah. Other categories included cosmetic restoration; unacceptable for dis-

Opposite: 1913 Mercer, with the famous T-head, 4-cyl. engine that brought many Mercers victories in the company's early years. Above: 1937 Hispano-Suiza.

play; and good restorable condition.

Harrah did not want all of his cars restored. The Rockefellers' 1907 convertible limousine was one such vehicle. "It's beautiful the way it is. The paint is old and faded and the brass is tarnished, but it's just a beautiful thing. … It's more beautiful than a restored one 'cause it just has aged gracefully."

While he never worked on his cars,

Harrah set the priorities and made the final approvals on each restoration. "One of the things I enjoy most is deciding what cars we're going to restore. I change my mind all the time." After the shop had finished with a car, Harrah test-drove it along Interstate 80 to see how it handled and if it could reach the manufacturer's advertised speeds. Forty percent of the cars he test-drove he sent back to his shop for further work.

Realizing research's vital role in the restoration process, Harrah bought all the original car literature his staff could find. He bragged that his library, which he formally started in 1959, had 99.9 percent of all early trade journals—the earliest on file was an 1895 Horseless Age magazine. Just prior to his death in 1978, he called it the second best library in the world, but didn't name the library that beat out his.

An automotive literature junky, Harrah read two to three automotive publications each night from a stack of information his library staff supplied him. It was this avid interest that made the library the complete archival automobile resource it is today.

In 1981, the library was appraised at $3.7 million and donated intact by the Holiday Corporation to the National Automobile Museum (The Harrah Collection). It houses owner, shop and restoration manuals; photographs; technical books; magazines from throughout the world; sales literature; wiring diagrams; upholstery samples; paint color chips and formulas; and much more.

Today, the museum's library serves car enthusiasts worldwide. For a minimal fee, the library's staff will answer specific questions and photocopy documents. To request research, log on to www.automuseum.org or call the museum at (775) 333-9300 for a research request form.

HARRAH'S LOVE OF SPEED

Harrah lived in the fast lane. Six wives. Casino magnate. And plenty of fast cars. Harrah once said that the car that best reflected his personality was a 12-cylinder Ferrari. He counted himself a friend of Enzo Ferrari, who "drove perfectly." Despite never racing, Harrah had been known to drive his Ferrari from Reno to Lake Tahoe on windy mountain roads at speeds up to 115 miles per hour.

His cars had to be fast. His philosophy on speed was "with speed you have superiority. My car'll go 150, and yours'll only go 140." He pressed his shop staff to

1960 Flying Caduceus Streamliner Jet-Powered Car.

create the "Jerrari"—a 1977 Jeep Wagoneer rebuilt with a DOHC Ferrari 365 GTC/4 V12 engine and C4 five-speed transmission—because he wanted a four-wheel drive sports car. He also enjoyed driving the 1909 Thomas, 1913 Mercer Raceabout and Stutz DV-32. He especially liked driving the 1908 Stearns that he called "a 90 mile-an-hour car, a real swinging car."

When Harrah died unexpectedly in June 1978, there were 50 cars still on his wish list. His plans for a new 600,000-square-foot automobile museum on the land he purchased next to Interstate 80 were scrapped, and the future of his automobile collection became imperiled. Harrah, the consummate gambler, did not make provisions in his will to save his collection. Some believe that Harrah didn't want to impose his passion on his corporation once he died.

Three years after his death, Holiday Corporation—which bought Harrah's Hotel/Casinos and the automobile collection in 1980—made the decision to sell-off the cars, which at that time were valued at $30 million. A mad dash ensued by car enthusiasts, the state of Nevada and the City of Reno to save the collection. The newly formed Harrah Automobile Foundation worked with the Holiday Corporation on the donation of 175 cars and the complete research library to create the National Automobile Museum (The Harrah Collection). The bulk donation was selected to accurately represent automobile history from inception through the 1970s. At that time, Holiday's donation of $25 million became the largest corporate philanthropic gift ever made.

THE HARRAH COLLECTION TODAY

In November 1989 the National Automobile Museum (The Harrah Collection) opened two blocks away from Harrah's Reno Hotel/Casino. Just outside Harrah's shadow, this museum thrives alongside the Truckee River.

Speculators mourned the death of the old Harrah's Automobile Collection prematurely. While some of the collection's gems had indeed been sold-off, Holiday had donated many premium automobiles. Favorites remained like the 1937 Hispano-Suiza Type J 12 Berline, a 1911 Franklin Averell Special Speed Car, Al Jolson's 16-cylinder 1933 Cadillac Series 452C All Weather Phaeton; a dual-cowl Chrysler Newport—one of six—bought in 1941 by the owner of the New York Yankees; Harrah's favored 1913 Mercer Series J, Type 35 Raceabout; a 1913 Stutz Series B Bearcat and Buck-

Also in the museum is this 1925 Julian Sport Coupe/Fleetwood with Serial No. 1 Radial Engine mounted in the rear. There was only one built.

minster Fuller's weird 1934 Dymaxion.

Make no mistake—this is a museum for both the car buff and the person who merely drives them. Unlike Harrah's Automobile Collection with its overwhelming rows of cars packed into three warehouses, the National Automobile Museum (The Harrah Collection) showcases its cars in the context of

how this invention has shaped people's lives and changed society forever.

"When you visit here, it's a step back in time," says executive director Jackie Frady. "This museum captures a whole era around the automobile—not just of the automobile."

This striking 105,000 square-foot facility, which holds more than 220 cars

dating from 1892 to the present, was said to have set the standard for automobile museum design worldwide when it opened. Its outside appearance salutes the automobile with its rounded metal-skinned exterior in heather fire mist—a popular 1950s car color—and chrome trim accents. Inside, the cars are divided into four galleries—one for

each quarter of the 20th century—along with corresponding street scenes complete with facades, street sounds and memorabilia from each era. Timelines document the progress of the automobile alongside the evolution of American society.

The strength of this museum is in its many rare, experimental and one-of-a-kind automobiles. On permanent exhibit, the 1906 Adams-Farwell 6A Convertible Runabout, one of 52 built, is the only one known to exist. Its amenities include an air-cooled rotary engine and pedal steering that could be installed at either the front or rear seats. Meanwhile, one of the most radically different American cars ever made also has its place here: the 1925 Julian Sport Coupe prototype. It features an air-cooled, twin-row, six-cylinder radial design engine mounted in the rear of the vehicle; a tubular backbone frame; and rear swing axles.

Another famous car, the 1907 Thomas Flyer "35," holds two distinguished titles. It is the winner of the 1908 New York-to-Paris race, and it is the museum's most highly prized historical automobile. Amazingly enough, the Thomas Flyer "35" was removed from its showroom floor just six days before the start of this famous race. Its body and fenders were fitted to accommodate extra gas tanks, coils of rope and spare tires. This rugged Thomas, with its 72-hp six-cylinder engine, came in first place after traveling 13,341 miles from New York to Paris by way of Manchuria and Siberia. It made the "impossible" journey in a mere 170 days.

This 1972 McLaren M20 Can-Am Race Car represented the high mark of the Can-Am McLarens. This factory team car was driven by Denny Hulme in 1972; Hulme won his last Can-Am race at Watkins Glen and finished 2nd in the Can-Am Championship in 1972 in the M20

Street scenes set the stage for the cars displayed in adjoining galleries while giving the visitor a feel for every era. Each car on display features a plaque with information on the model, engine, builder, price when new, stroke, bore, displacement and a short historical narrative. At times, the individual car's past is also included.

The turn-of-the-century street covers the period between 1900 and 1925. Hands-on exhibits give visitors the touch, sounds and sights of this era from the stiff and laborious Model T hand-crank and the obnoxious bulb horn to stereoscopes that feature street scenes and fashionable clothing from the turn of the 20th Century.

Visitors enter Gallery One through a blacksmith's shop, illustrating the changing reliance from horse-drawn carriages to cars. One of the world's finest collections of horseless carriages can be found here, including the marvelous 1892 Phil-

ion. In addition, many first-year production vehicles—such as the 1903 Ford Model A with a rear entrance tonneau and the 1903 Cadillac Model A Runabout—are here as well. Besides cars, visitors can view the Bowser Self-Measuring Oil Tank and vintage clothing and jewelry from that era.

The 1930s street captures the era with its art deco hotel and Palace Theatre facades, and a new-fangled invention called the television set. Conjuring up the

days prior to billboards, the street is dotted with Burma Shave advertising signs.

Gallery Two showcases the era's heyday of automobile experimentation from a papier-mâché car to battery- and steam-powered automobiles. The odd 1937 Airmobile Experimental Sedan features three wheels, front-wheel drive and a bumper resembling a fish's fin. This gallery of extremes lets visitors glimpse at the practical 1921 Ford "T" Kampkar—the world's first

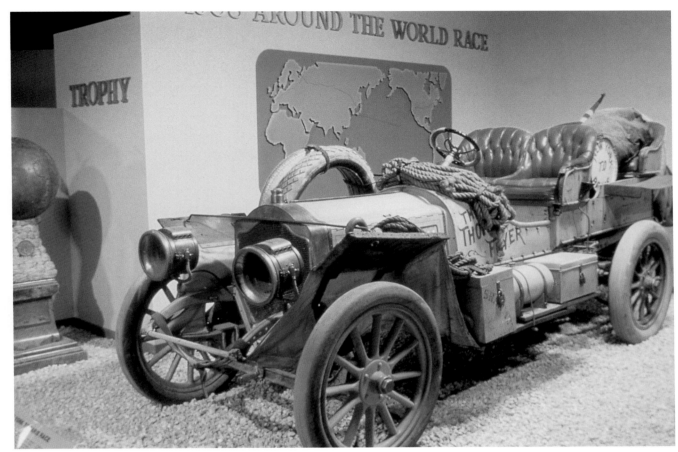

AROUND THE WORLD RACE

TROPHY

1907 Thomas Flyer, a New York-to-Paris race winner in its day. The Harrahs brought George Schuster, the car's only race-distance driver, to Reno to help in its authentic restoration.

Visitors stroll through the garage of a suburban 1950s house to get into Gallery Four. Here are the collection's racecars, vehicles from the 1960s and '70s and one of the changing exhibit venues, the Masterpiece Circle. The 1960 Flying Caduces—the first jet-propulsion land speed car—is a bright red behemoth that raced on the Bonneville Salt Flats in Utah. Other notable racecars displayed here include the 1972 McLaren M20 Can-Am car and the 1955 Kurtis Indy car. Also exhibited are Elvis' 1973 Cadillac, Harrah's "Jerrari," a 1981 24-carat-gold De Lorean and Frank Sinatra's 1961 L. 6.4 Ghia.

The museum, which completed its capital campaign last year and fully paid off its construction debt, has established a $1 million endowment which will continue to grow to ensure its future. As the National Automobile Museum (The Harrah Collection) evolves through its changing exhibits, it continues to seek museum-quality vehicles and new trend-setting cars to keep displays fresh for returning guests.

Bill Harrah believed that his collection would be self-supporting one day. Today, many of his cars are preserved for future generations to enjoy. During a Motor Trend interview in 1969, Harrah talked about how he hoped the cars he restored would be around far into the future. "Two hundred years from now, I hope the cars will still exist, so I can look down on them and say, 'Well, by God, I saved those cars from oblivion.'"

Harrah must be smiling down on the National Automobile Museum (The Harrah Collection). ◨◧

recreational vehicle—and the exquisite 1921 Rolls-Royce Silver Ghost covered in copper sheeting and highlighted with rich wood trim carved from makash ebony. Visitors can also check out the 1923 copper-cooled Chevrolet engine—the smallest ever produced by Chevrolet—and a 1924 Willys-Knight sleeve valve engine with four cylinders.

The neighboring 1950s to 1970s street highlights society's shift from downtown to the suburbs. Empty storefront facades are soaped with the message "moved to mall," highlighting society's new mobility.

The repair bay of a 1950s Union 76 gas station holds the portal to Gallery Three where the museum's classic automobiles are on exhibit. The elegant 1936 Mercedes-Benz Type 500K Special Roadster with Sindelfingen coachwork is the most expensive car in the collection today. Another jewel here is the ahead-of-its-time 1938 Phantom Corsair that sports an aerodynamic body, front-wheel drive, electric gearshift and a Cord V8 Lycoming engine. The 1948 Tucker engine—a modified six-cylinder version of an air-cooled Franklin aircraft engine—can also be viewed, as well as a Tucker car.

The last of the street scenes, the Modern Street, features a mall front, groomed tree-lined avenue and freeway photos.

Stirling moss

The Champion Without A Crown

"S tirling Moss is my all-time hero," asserts three-time World Motor Racing champion, Jackie Stewart. "He was always the consummate professional." During his all-too-short 15-year career, Moss drove 85 different cars, winning more than 40 percent of the 529 events he entered and was among the first Britons to drive racing cars for a living, racing on circuits worldwide. British motor racing in the early post-war period was a deadly game played out in cars with little thought to safety. Petrol tanks were placed over driver's legs, competitors wore linen T-shirts and simple crash hats, and seat belts weren't conceived of yet. Fatalities were common. "Part of the pleasure of motor racing in those days was its danger," reflects Stirling Moss. "If you removed the feeling of danger, you removed the feeling of achievement."

BY MIKE TAYLOR

Moss was impassioned about racing early in life, influenced by his father, who raced at Indianapolis and Brooklands, and his mother, who was active in trials and rallies. As a boy, his mother, Aileen, allowed Stirling to steer the family car along the drive of their home by the Thames. It was then that he recalls being exhilarated by speed.

Aged just 18, Moss's first opportunity to take part in motor sport came when he entered a local trial in 1947. Driving a pre-war BMW 328 bought by his father, the event gave him his first success. Early the following year, father and son passed the Cooper Car Co. showroom in Surbiton, South London, stopping to inspect a sleek Mk11

Cooper 500 racer. An order was placed and in his first event at the Prescott Hill Climb, Moss finished the day in fourth position in the 500cc class. Next came another hill climb, this time at Stanmer Park in Sussex, where he won. His first actual race was in Blackburn, Lancashire, in which he managed first in practice, fastest lap and first in the event. The die was cast.

"I think I was lucky to start my career in hill climbs because it helped me to develop my driving style," notes Moss. "I had no bad habits to break. It enabled me to set my own limits, though, being a very competitive person, track racing was where I wanted to be."

The following year Moss went to picturesque Lake Garda where he was

Barely licensed to drive, young Stirling attempted to spend his hard-earned equestrian prize money (he and sister Pat, above on horse, formed a formidable pair in the horse-competition circuit) on a race car—father Alfred was so angered (and alarmed at Stirling's flirtation with the dangerous sport of motor racing), he confiscated his son's Morgan (above, left). Alfred's anger soon wore off, however, loaning his newly purchased BMW 328 to Stirling for speed trials and hill climbs (above, top). The Cooper (above, bottom) came later.

The year was 1950 and Moss was just 21 when Hersham and Walton Motors (HWM) was in need of an extra driver for their team. For some at HWM, Moss was a wildcard, a young driver who was driving over his head. But once recruited, Moss's racing instinct surfaced, resulting in many wins and increased exposure and earnings.

clearly in his element, outperforming Mario Tadini, who drove a V12 Ferrari. Moss, in a Cooper JAP, finished third overall. Back in the U.K., Moss had the same result in the Madgwick Cup in September. During the end-of-season dinner celebration of the 500 Club,

Moss strengthened his friendship with Ken Gregory, which paid dividends later.

Moss's early success and cavalier style caught the attention of HWM. He was invited to drive for them in 1950; talented racer Lance Macklin joined the team in mid-year. Soon the

21-year-old Moss was racing, seeing the sights of Europe—and being paid for it.

During the Bari Grand Prix in Italy, Moss sustained his first accident. Amidst a full four-wheel drift, he was knocked off line by a back marker, his

car careening off the track, hitting a tree at 80 mph. Despite a broken kneecap and some missing front teeth, Moss jumped clear.

By September, Stirling had won eleven out of nineteen races and achieved a class lap record at Brands

Hatch. But, despite his busy schedule, trying to get a drive in the 1950 RAC Tourist Trophy race proved almost impossible. Luckily, help came in the form of family friend and racing journalist Tommy Wisdom, who arranged for Moss to drive a road-prepared Jaguar XK120. Wisdom's faith in Moss was vindicated when Moss set a new Dundrod lap record, winning the race in pouring rain.

When the Rouen event was over, Ferrari again made contact and suggested Moss should race for him during the winter period with a full Formula 1 drive in 1952. Not quite 22 at the time, it was a chance for the young driver to race with the world's elite team (next to Alfa Romeo's, according to Moss). Yet Ferrari clearly had other intentions, changing his mind at the last minute, a turn of

STIRLING STANDARD

Moss first crossed swords with Enzo Ferrari in 1951. The Italian race master offered Stirling a drive in both the Rouen and Bari Grands Prix. Moss was already committed to the first, accepting the second with alacrity. But for Ferrari, it was either both or neither.

events that birthed a difficult relationship with Ferrari. Both Stirling and father Alfred Moss opted to steer clear of Ferrari for the next ten years, as the Italian racing giant's brusque business tactics didn't gel with Moss's gentlemanly preference. Moss never did drive for Ferrari.

At the Le Mans 24-hour race that summer, Moss led for eight hours in a C-type Jaguar, breaking the lap record

Left: Moss's first drive at Monaco in the 500, 1950. Directly above: Moss set a new circuit record, winning the RAC Tourist Trophy race at Dundrod in pouring rain. Undeterred concentration is etched in his face, at speed in his Cooper (top) and in the Aston Martin DB3S at Goodwood, 1956 (opposite).

The first car to ever exceed 100 mph for seven straight days (and nights), the bronze XK120 Coupe was driven by the Jaguar works team trio consisting of (from left, atop car) Bert Hadley, Leslie Johnson and Moss. The team averaged 100.31 mph for 16,851 miles. Right: Moss with Fangio after Aintree; note a happy Pat Moss in front of policeman.

three times before being forced to retire when an oil pipe fractured.

Moss also took up rallying for Rootes, driving the less-than-sporting Sunbeam Talbot 90 in the 1952 Monte Carlo Rally, finishing second overall.

Meanwhile, Ken Gregory had become Moss's manager, learning the intricacies of high finance under the tutelage of Moss senior. By now young Moss was racing every weekend and testing throughout the week. His active racing

life ensured—indeed, demanded—that he keep fit, aided by a strict regime of non-drinking and only occasional smoking.

Now a member of the Jaguar works team, Moss enthusiastically took the

wheel of one of the three C-types entered for the 1952 Le Mans race, though all three cars retired due to overheating. However, Moss, together with Bert Hadley and Leslie Johnson, drove a Jaguar XK120 Coupé at

"Many times I am asked who I considered the most talented racing drivers of my time and I always think of you and Ascari—two people with the same kind of temperament. But whilst Alberto gave much importance to qualifying, reaching the corner and taking the lead, so that he was always way ahead of the other, you did not have such a rigid approach, but became a fighter who knew how to take the lead, even when all seemed lost."

—Five-time World Champion driver, Juan Manuel Fangio, in his foreword to Moss's autobiography

Montlhéry in August, covering 16,851 miles and averaging over 100 mph in an endurance test, an outstanding performance for men and machine.

In 1953 Moss had another shunt, this time at Silverstone, again driving a Jaguar C-type. Coming upon a slower machine at 100 mph, Moss lost control, luckily managing to escape unhurt. In the gruelling Le Mans, sharing the C-type driving duties with Peter Collins, Moss managed a creditable second place. The year was brought to a premature close however, when, driving a Cooper JAP at Castle Combe Moss outbraked Tony Rolt's Connaught, only to be punted from behind, which sent him somersaulting spectacularly off the track. The result was three

The Maserati 250F helped springboard Moss to top-level victories; he drove the 250F in his first Monaco and Italian Grands Prix in 1955. Moss noted once: "We chose the Maserati, and it proved to be a beautiful, stable, lovely car to drive ... It was just a pity it was not more reliable." ·

months of recuperation. As for rallying, again Moss entered the Monte in January driving another Talbot 90, finishing sixth overall. Better was to come in the Alpine Rally later when he gained a creditable outright win and a Coupe des Alpes in the Talbot-based Alpine two-seater.

Towards year's end, father Alfred and manager Gregory were in discussion over a suitable car for their protégé to drive in '54. Overtures to Mercedes met with a polite but firm "no." The only alternative was to buy, and an order was placed with Maserati for a 250F.

The Maserati outstripped almost every car in which Moss had previously raced. After winning the Daily Mail Trophy race at Aintree, he raced in the Italian Grand Prix, leading until lap 78 when his oil tank split, forcing him to retire. As compensation Pirelli gave him a winner's bonus and Fangio recommended him as the "moral victor."

In August 1954, Moss won his first Formula 1 race at Oulton Park driving the 250F. "The 250F was a super car to drive, very user-friendly but sadly not as strong or reliable as the Ferrari," comments Moss.

Later, for the final Swiss Grand Prix at Berne, Moss put the 250F on pole—much to the chagrin of Mercedes. Better yet, he led the Mercedes team in the Italian Grand Prix until lubrication difficulties prevented him from certain victory. This did not go unnoticed by Mercedes. A cable from Alfred Neubauer, the charismatic Mercedes team manager, sealed a deal, hiring Moss as a member of the Mercedes works team for the following year.

An important event in the race calendar of 1955 was the Mille Miglia held in May, a race that caused many a driver (Moss included) considerable concern. Of critical importance was the sheer variety—and speed capabilities—of the entrants and the undeniable fact that the locals knew the tricky course more intimately than the outsiders. For this event the colorful and experienced motoring journalist Denis 'Jenks' Jenkinson was to sit alongside Moss with route direction hand signals, reading from his special note contraption.

The 300SLR open sports car was based on a space-frame chassis and powered by a 3-litre straight-8 engine that produced a fearsome 300 bhp.

Starting and ending in Brescia, the pair had just two days to traverse the 1,000-mile course. Reaching speeds of 170 mph they averaged just under 100 mph for the 992.329 miles. It was a truly outstanding performance. Enduring heat, crowds and negotiating

Racing on the Mercedes works team meant driving the number-two car behind the legendary Fangio. The experience also developed a friendship between Moss and Fangio, shown here at the Nurburgring in 1955.

markedly slower entrants, Moss and 'Jenks' took a well-deserved flag. "The SLR was just right for the Mille Miglia," says Moss emphatically. "It wasn't an easy car to drive, but it was very competent for that event."

Moss paired up with Peter Collins in

one of three Mercedes 300SLRs entered for the 600-mile, 13-lap Sicilian Targa Florio in October 1955. Moss started the race but, on lap four and in the lead, he careened off the course and dropped some 12 feet onto uneven ground below. In a lesser car, and possibly a lesser driver, it would have spelled disaster. But masterful handiwork pushed the car back onto the track and Moss was back in the race. When he handed over to Collins there was some time to make up and a lead to recapture. By the time Collins handed back to Moss he'd achieved it.

Moss then expanded the gap, finishing 5 minutes ahead of teammates Juan Manuel Fangio and Karl Kling, posting a fastest lap of 43 minutes 7.4 seconds. However, it was to be a hollow victory, for at the subsequent press conference Mercedes announced their withdrawal from all forms of competitive motor sport, bringing the glorious 300SLR campaign to a close.

For Moss the news created a dilemma: What would he race in 1956? The answer quickly narrowed to three options. In the U.K., work was proceeding on a new car sponsored by industrialist Tony Vandervell. Called the Vanwall, the car featured a chassis and suspension designed by Colin Chapman and a stylish body shaped by aircraft aerodynamicist Frank Costin. The 4-cylinder 2.5-liter engine was designed by Norton motorcycle engineer Leo Kuzmicki. Moss's second alternative was the BRM out of the Owen Racing Organisation, while third was the Connought. Financed by the building fraternity McAlpine, the car had been re-designed into a Formula 1 machine with a reworked power unit.

On a cold but sunny day in late November, all three cars were brought to Silverstone for Moss to try. Both the BRM and Connaught performed almost identically with Moss returning lap times similar to those he'd achieved in his Maserati. The Vanwall, however, proved to be markedly quicker, Moss shaving 3 seconds off the 1 minute 50 second times of the other two cars. Yet, despite his patriotism, his gut feeling led him back to Modena, and Maserati. In early 1956 Moss was in New Zealand for the Grand Prix, where he gained pole position, won the race and set a lap record driving the Maserati 250F.

He also had the opportunity to drive the Vanwall in its debut race at Silverstone where he was matched against Hawthorn in the BRM. It was a notable first outing: pole position, fastest lap and first home. In the Mille Miglia, Moss again teamed up with Jenkinson, though their efforts would not be rewarded when their Maserati 350S came to rest against a line of trees, stopping just shy of a 300-foot drop.

The following year was an eventful one for Moss, filled with ups and downs. For the 1957 Le Mans race, Frank Costin was drafted to produce a coupe version of the Maserati, the work contracted to Zagato. Unfortunately, the combination of Costin's design work with the Italian company's interpretation did not gel. Fangio wisely opted to drive an open car while Harry Schell partnered Moss in the coupe. It proved the wrong choice for Moss; the open car was faster and ultimately more reliable, the coupe breaking its final drive while lying second. Moss did, however, win the British Grand Prix driving a Vanwall that year, swapping cars mid-race with Tony Brooks.

Away from the tracks, MG approached Moss over making a new attempt on the class F record at Bonneville Salt Flats, Utah. In a beautifully sleek car powered by a supercharged 1500cc twin-cam engine producing 290 bhp, Moss set new records of 245 mph for 1 mile and 224 mph for 10 miles.

Moss met Rob Walker in Casablanca in October 1957, and the two men struck a deal—Moss would now drive for Walker Racing. As early as November, Moss entered the Venezuelan Grand Prix in his Maserati 450S. Reminiscent of the Silverstone incident just four years prior, history repeated itself when a slower car got in the way, in this case an AC Ace. Moss emerged bruised, but alive—the Ace driver died.

In 1958 Stirling got behind the wheel of a Climax-engined Cooper for Walker; the first race was in Buenos Aires in January. Against the might of the full Ferrari works team, Moss managed an outright win—despite having no clutch, making 'crash' gearbox changes, and with tires worn to the canvas.

Next month, in the Cuban Grand Prix, Moss was in a Ferrari 335. It was to be an eventful venue: Fangio was kidnapped under the orders of Fidel Castro while, sadly, a local driver crashed into the crowd, killing five spectators. The organizers stopped the race—or so they thought. Because the flags had not been waved at the start line, they were invalid. And Moss, in second at the time, sped over the line, passed Master Gregory, and claimed victory.

Soon thereafter, finding himself with no factory Maserati on offer and not being one to sit on his hands, he went to the people at Newport Pagnell, the team being managed by the capable John Wyer. By this time, Aston Martin was campaigning the DBR1. In Moss's hands AM enjoyed victories at Nurburgring, the RAC Tourist Trophy, the British Empire Trophy, and the Sussex Trophy that year.

Driving for Vanwall, an initial three-car entry in the Monaco Grand Prix proved unfruitful as none reached the finishing line, Moss's car lasting only until lap 38. The Portuguese Grand Prix was a different story. After gaining pole on the grid, Moss passed Mike Hawthorn, who was trying to push-start his car uphill, not far from the chequered flag. Moss shouted "Turn it around!" Hawthorn did so, and came in second, only to be disqualified. In true Moss style he stood up saying Hawthorn was within the regulations since he had not actually pushed his car on the track. The judges relented.

The last race of the season was in Casablanca, a demanding circuit where sand often blew from the dunes onto the track. Moss knew he needed at least a win to get the championship. Three Vanwalls and three Ferraris faced each other across the grid. Moss led from start to finish, but Hawthorn came in second, resulting in Moss failing to get the cup. Had Moss not spoken up for Hawthorn at Portugal he would have gained the World Championship by a margin of some six points. But that was not the way Moss operated. Vanwall did at least win the Constructor's Championship. "The Vanwall was not a nice car to drive, but it achieved its goal, to win the championship," recalls Moss.

In 1959 Moss was awarded the OBE (Order of the British Empire), and work began in earnest developing the 2.5-liter Cooper Climax (though gearbox choice was limited by the rear-engined design). By Monaco, the Cooper was ready. But during lap 81 the transmission failed, as

"Movement is tranquility."–Stirling Moss

it did again at Zandvoort.

At the Nurburgring Moss was sharing the honours with Jack Fairman in an Aston DBR1. After Fairman slid off the track, losing time, Moss got the hand-off and drove an

> "Moss not only is a slight, balding Englishman with an eye towards money, women and fine racing cars; Moss is the quickest way through a corner, the fastest way around the course and the ultimate performance of any racing machine. Moss is either victory or mechanical destruction ..."
>
> —*Dennis Shattuck for* Road & Track, *1960*

perate. Moss's injuries were not dreadfully serious and he missed only two races. He rejoined the Formula 1 tour in Portugal only to be disqualified for pushing his car, replicating the Hawthorn saga of two years before.

In the 1961 Monaco Grand Prix, again behind the wheel of the Climax-engined Lotus 18, Moss held off the entire Ferrari works team to take the flag. The win occurred despite a quick weld repair job to the chassis while the car was on the grid, fuelled up and ready. To overcome heat exhaustion, side panels were removed to increase air circulation while Moss covered himself in cold water.

Moss had thoroughly trounced the Ferrari team in a previous year's car, producing lap times of within a second of his pole position performance, giving the now famous Moss wave to the approving crowds. To many it was one of Moss's most memorable drives, the three shark-nosed red Ferraris taking turns at snapping at his exhaust pipe lap after lap.

At the Nurburgring, Moss again proved the impossible possible (or even the unimaginable imaginable). Opting for Dunlop racing tires, his hunch of rain was later vindicated, though not for long—the racing rubber became hotter

Opposite: Moss at the Bonneville Salt Flats. Above, top: Moss spins out of control at Spa, 1960; his wrecked Lotus 18 below. That year, Moss marked up 20 wins, one of which was the Monaco Grand Prix (above, right).

extraordinary race, winning by 41 seconds. Moss was less lucky at Le Mans, when the engine of his Aston Martin DBR1 dropped a valve. In the RAC Tourist Trophy event he borrowed the Fairman/Shelby Aston to take the flag, giving Aston Martin the Constructor's Championship.

Back in the streets of the Monaco Principality in 1960, Moss took the winner's flag driving a Lotus 18. The win was remarkable when it was discovered that the engine mountings had broken, the power unit hanging by its water pipes and cables.

Mid-year that year, disaster struck at Spa when, during practice, Moss in the Lotus 18 went into a skid, the car hit the banking and Moss was flung out. He was taken to a hospital and flown back to the U.K. the following day to recu-

Goodwood, 1962: The crash that ended Moss's professional racing career, as it happened (above, top), before he was wrenched free of his Lotus (right), and the wreckage left behind. The cause of the crash remains a mystery.

by the lap as the track dried out. Yet Moss pressed home to victory, a full 20.4 seconds ahead of Wolfgang von Tripps' Ferrari.

Moss was invited into discussions with Ferrari for the '62 season. What emerged was an arrangement whereby a car would be loaned to Walker for Moss to drive. It was an astute deal: Ferrari got the best driver and Walker got the best car. But the Ferrari was late in arriving, so an alternative was sought for the Glover Trophy Race at Goodwood.

Significantly, Moss opted for the faithful Lotus 18, now fitted with a V8 Coventry Climax engine, updated to partial '62 specification. Moss placed the car on the pole alongside Graham Hill and Jim Clark. As the race progressed, Moss began experiencing gear-selector problems and was forced to make a pit stop. By the time he was out again, Hill was already two laps ahead. Intent on making up time, Moss set the fastest lap time.

As Moss and Hill approached St. Mary's, a remote section of the Goodwood track, a marshal was seen to give a less-than-clear signal to Hill of Moss's approaching position behind. Hill, however, moved into Moss's path, forcing him off the track and onto the grass. The car appeared to hit something, the jolt making Moss seem as though he was ejecting from his seat. The impact caused the distributor cap to become dislodged and flames to shoot from the exhaust; the car came to rest in a ditch.

Moss's racing resumé qualifies him as an all-time great: In his Grand Prix career, he raced 66 times with 16 poles, 16 wins and 20 fastest laps. Moss also won the Mille Miglia in 1955 with Denis Jenkinson. His quest for the World Championship included finishing 12th, 3rd three times, and 2nd four times—all in consecutive years from 1954 through 1961.

"I don't recall anything of the race, the pit stops or the accident," says Moss.

Moss was seriously hurt and did not regain consciousness for 38 days. His injuries included damage to the left side of his body and brain. Gradually, however, he began to make progress and to test the possibility of returning to the sport he loved.

Moss went to Goodwood in May 1963 to drive a Lotus 19. Resplendent in blue overalls and sporting a beard, it seemed Moss had lost none of his magic. But to the man himself his drive was depressingly lackluster, bereft of the talent and flare that had made him a household name. Sadly, he announced his retirement.

But was his decision to retire premature? Speculating about that trying period, there's no doubt in Moss's mind. "Looking back, perhaps I made a hasty decision, but I had huge pressure from the press. Given time I think my concentration would have returned and I could have adapted my driving style to disc brakes and later to slick tires. And this did not concern me for the first few years after retirement; knowing I was the fastest was some consolation."

And so at the age of 32 Moss took on a new career, that of public relations manager for sponsors ShellMex-BP. As a recognized PR asset, his role evolved into promoting the man he knew best, Stirling Moss. His celebrity, particularly among the British, culminated at his knighting ceremony in 2000, exemplifying his country's love affair with the racing star.

British National Champion ten times, "Sir Stirling" is clearly sad to never have won a World Championship, yet is consoled with the knowledge that he was always considered the driver to beat "I believe what makes a great racing driver is versatility and consistency, and respect for other drivers." Loved and respected still, few men share Moss's honor of becoming a legend in one's own lifetime. AQ

The MOSS Family Racing Tradition

Like Father (and Mother), Like Son (and Daughter)

They say it's all in the genes, and Stirling Moss's parents certainly had motor sport coursing through their veins. At the dawn of the 1920s, Alfred Moss made his sporting debut with a fearsome device known as an AV Bicar, a tandem-seated cyclecar powered by a 1000cc air-cooled vee-twin engine hung so far out at the rear that the lack of weight on the front wheels made cornering a real adventure.

BY DAVID BURGESS-WISE

Nevertheless, Moss vied with the best right from the start. In the Essex Motor Club Winter Trial in February 1921 he faced such notables as Archie Frazer-Nash, Ivy Cummings and Douglas Hawkes. Another entrant who would play a notable role in the career of the motoring Mosses was ex-Royal Flying Corps ace Donald Marendaz, driving a Marseal car of his own design.

Despite the design shortcomings of the AV, Moss completed the course, but was then disqualified for leaving the designated route. But he had little option, for a rear tire had burst twice, and he had to drive to the nearest village on the rim to find a replacement.

The unsatisfactory AV soon gave way to a GN cyclecar. In the GN, Moss won a gold medal at the Junior Car Club's testing London-Manchester Run in April 1921. A few weeks later, Moss and the GN were among the finishers in the 336-mile London-Holyhead Trial.

Racing at Brooklands was the next step, and Alfred Moss entered his GN for the Novice's Handicap at the Spring Meeting of the JCC on 28 May and came third in the one-lap race behind a Bugatti and a Silver Hawk.

The GN brought success in hillclimbing, too: at South Harting in June, Moss made third fastest time in the two-seater touring class.

The following season seems to have been a quiet one for Moss, but then he acquired a 1496cc Anzani-engined Crouch "Le Mans" sports car, named for the venue of the 1922 International Light Car Race in which a similar car had finished fourth. Moss's Crouch had stylish polished aluminum bodywork with an "airship tail." It made its race debut in March 1923 during the Junior Car Club's Annual Trial, which, after a short road run, featured competitive events on the Brooklands track and test hill.

Alfred Moss began with the AV Bicar (above) before moving to the GN (below). He raced his Crouch "Le Mans" at Brooklands (upper right) and in public road speed events (lower right).

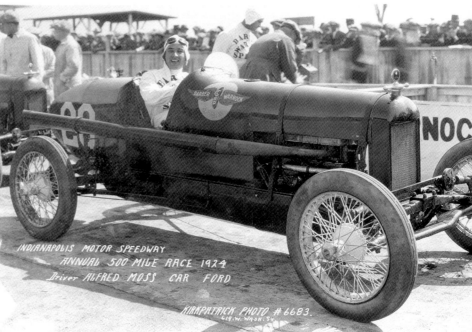

INDIANAPOLIS MOTOR SPEEDWAY
ANNUAL 500 MILE RACE 1924
Driver ALFRED MOSS CAR FORD

KIRKPATRICK PHOTO #6683.
219.W. WASH. ST.

Brooklands success with the Crouch (above left) was Alfred Moss's stepping stone to a drive at Indianapolis in 1924 in a Barber-Warnock Ford (above right). The referee that year was Henry Ford, seen here trying a Barber-Warnock on for size, watched by Barney Oldfield (behind Henry) and son Edsel (center, with trilby hat).

Moss was "very good" in the acceleration test and made fastest flying lap at 61.64 mph. In the afternoon two-lap handicap race, he started on scratch. Though he was unable to catch the more favorably handicapped GNs which finished 1-2, he came second in Class 5 and fourth in the overall classification behind well-known Brooklands racers E.B. Ware (Morgan), Archie Frazer-Nash (GN) and D. Chinery (Gwynne 8).

Moss, who won the Private Competitors' Handicap at the Easter 1923 Brooklands meeting, was now racing against the top amateurs like Malcolm Campbell, George Eyston and Woolf Barnato.

There was another win at the Brooklands Autumn meeting when the Crouch—by now enough of a veteran to be known as "Grandpa"—won the 75 mph Short Handicap at 71.25 mph.

An end-of-season highlight at Brooklands was the 200-Mile Race in mid-October, run as separate events for 1100cc and 1500cc cars. The Crouch competed in the afternoon 1500cc event, which suffered from an excess of non-starters, though there were still "sufficient cars … to make a really good race." But not for Alfred Moss. After 29 laps he and his mechanic pushed the Crouch into the pits with a blown head gasket after a "terrific battle" with Parry Thomas's Marlborough-Thomas.

After a relatively successful season, Alfred Moss had his sights set high, his son Stirling told me: "Dad's great

ambition was to race in the Indianapolis 500. He was training to be a dentist, and he told my grandfather, 'I want to study in Indianapolis, because that's where the best dental bridgework is done. But it is a bit expensive.'

"So my grandfather, thinking Dad was solely going over to [attend the] university, said: 'Well, I'll sponsor you to go there.'

"Well, of course Dad did learn some dentistry, but his main reason for going was to race! Getting a drive at Indianapolis wasn't that easy, but he had a letter of introduction from a British motor agent and went to see Louis Chevrolet.

"My father gave him his letter and Chevrolet put it down on the table. Dad noticed he'd put some papers on top of it and went away knowing he'd left the letter behind.

"My father called back later and said he'd left his letter of introduction. Of course they couldn't find it, so Louis Chevrolet said: 'I suppose you know what your letter said; if you would like to dictate it to my secretary, I'll sign it.'

"So my father dictated a far more elaborate letter—'Alfred Moss really is a fantastic driver, signed Louis Chevrolet'—which was very useful to him!"

Armed with Chevrolet's letter, Moss talked his way into the 1924 Indy 500 race team run by local Ford dealer Barber-Warnock. A 2-liter eight-valve Barber-Warnock Fronty-Ford built by the

The Model T Ford ancestry of the Barber-Warnock (top, in the Indy pit lane) is revealed by its transverse front suspension. Standing behind Harry Harder's Barber-Warnock Special (bottom) are the team members, including Alfred Moss, second from right.

Alfred Moss's garage at Thornton Heath (above right) operated a carrier pigeon service (above, left) which helped rescue stranded motorists in pre-cellphone days. Aileen Moss (below) helps push-start son Stirling's Maserati 250F in a muddy postwar paddock.

Chevrolet brothers had come fifth in the 500 in 1923, and the Barber-Warnock company had entered a three-car team for the 1924 race. Preparation of the B-W Fords was meticulous—every nut and bolt was welded in place by the Chevrolets' mechanic "Skinny" Clemons—and all three cars finished. Moss came in 16th, outlasting such Indy greats as Eddie Hearne, Joe Boyer and two-times winner Tommy Milton, all of whom failed to cover the distance.

While he was in Indianapolis, Moss also competed on local dirt tracks, driving cars like Skinny Clemons' "Dixon's Graphite Special." He returned to Britain in 1925 as a qualified dentist with inside knowledge of race car preparation and a Frontenac distributorship.

In partnership with his brother-in-law, Moss opened a garage in the South London suburb of Thornton Heath, with agencies for the popular Crossley and Rover marques. He built himself a Fronty-Ford-Speedsport on a cut-and-shut Model T chassis: it won the 75-mph Short Handicap at the 1925 Brooklands August Bank Holiday Meeting.

An ingenious man, Moss equipped his breakdown truck—a large and ancient Fiat—with carrier pigeons to send messages back to the garage in case spares were urgently needed to make roadside repairs. Nevertheless, after a couple of years he bowed out of the garage business and returned to dentistry, establishing a highly successful

Aileen Moss drove this short-chassis Marendaz Special with aplomb in trials and rallies during 1936. The Mosses also took their infant son Stirling to Brooklands around this time; he still recalls burning his stomach on a hot exhaust pipe when incautiously looking into a racer's cockpit in the Paddock!

chain of dental surgeries which would ultimately become Britain's biggest.

There was a reason for the change of focus. In 1927 he had married a young Scotswoman named Aileen Craufurd. The couple had met when she was spectating at Brooklands, her passion for motoring stemming from her time driving a Crossley ambulance for the Royal Flying Corps during World War I.

Moss gave up racing after he married, but some while after Stirling was born in 1929 Aileen began driving in trials and rallies, eventually becoming Ladies' Trials Champion. Moss owned a 1932 Marendaz Special built by his old racing rival Captain D.M.K.Marendaz and in 1934 he and Aileen drove it in the RAC Rally as members of the Maren-

daz works team. Aileen Moss was only one of many competitors who hit the wooden barriers in the tricky driving tests on the Bournemouth seafront in the final stage, and the Mosses finished a lowly 79th in class.

At the beginning of 1935, soon after the birth of their daughter Pat, Aileen bought a new Singer sports car, one of just 71 examples of the six-cylinder Le Mans model to be built. Feeling that her birth date, the seventh of the month, was lucky, she had it registered "CPD 7." The gesture (and her spirited driving) rewarded her with a Starting Control Award in the Singer MCC Midland rally in April and second place in class in the Scottish Rally the following month.

The next year, Aileen was back at the

wheel of a Marendaz Special, this time a new 1936 short-chassis two-seater registered "DPG 7" which was subsequently fitted with a Zoller supercharger. A third-class award in the Coventry Cup Trial in March started the season well, followed by a fine performance in the RAC Rally at the beginning of April. After hitting the curb while setting a blisteringly fast time in the first driving test, she made the best time of the entire entry in the tricky hill-climbing test and finished sixth in class. A few days later, she won a special award in the Lancashire & Cheshire Sporting Trial. Although Alfred was usually content to occupy the passenger seat when Aileen was competing—he entered his old black Marendaz along-

side her white car in the Blackpool Rally in June, but the awards eluded both husband and wife.

Aileen lost a front tire in the Scottish rally in June, won a silver medal in the Torquay Trial and Rally in July and took a first class award in the August Barnstaple Trial.

And Alfred brought the 1936 season—and, it seems, the couple's active sporting career—to a close by winning a silver medal in the 59-mile MCC Buxton Trial in November.

Opting for a more comfortable motoring life, the next year Alfred bought himself a new Bentley with Park Ward saloon bodywork. And expressed himself bitterly disappointed when it wouldn't quite reach 100 mph. ▲○

Pat Moss

A Legend in Her Own Right

Pat Moss-Carlsson, one of the most illustrious names in international motorsport, had one advantage in her distinguished career as a rally driver. And that was a big one. She had been taught to drive by her big brother Stirling.

She is like her brother in many ways. She has an outgoing personality, is friendly with the press, has a good sense of humor and is tremendously competitive. Pat had two major sporting talents—driving and horse-show jumping—but with her brother's help, the "driving bug" finally won out.

She started riding at age 3 and show-jumped horses in international events for several years before turning seriously to cars. While riding, she met British royalty along the way, and would meet more royalty later on during awards ceremonies in her rally career. Monaco's Prince Rainier and Princess Grace were frequent "donors" at Monte Carlo Rally trophy programs.

Pat, who was married to the legendary Swedish rally star Erik Carlsson in 1963 (their daughter Susie is also an equestrienne), won the Monte Carlo Rally "Coupe des Dames" trophy a remarkable nine times and came in third over-all in 1965. But collecting the women's division trophies was no big deal to Pat Moss-Carlsson. "Sure, winning the women's part was okay," she once said, "but I wanted to beat the men. My goal was to score outright wins."

One of the best rally drivers in the world, she achieved that distinction when she won the lengthy and incredibly difficult Liege-Rome-Liege Marathon Rally in 1960 aboard a big Austin-Healy 3000. Her navigator was Ann Wisdom, and their drive marked the first time that a women's team had scored an outright victory in an international rally. Pat would win three more—the Dutch Tulip and the German Rally in 1962, and the Italian Sestrieres in 1968.

During her 15 years of rallying at the top, she was guided primarily by two navigators (or co-drivers as they are called today): England's Ann Wisdom and Sweden's Liz Nystrom. She drove for the British Motor Corporation (BMC), Ford, Saab, Lancia and Alpine Renault.

In addition to her four outright wins, a few other career highlights include a second place overall in Britain's 1961 RAC Rally; a third overall in the 1962 East African Safari and 1965 Monte Carlo Rally; a second overall in the 1968 Italian San Remo; a second overall in the 1962 Polish Rally; and a third overall in the 1967 Czech Rally.

— Randy Barnett

One of the rare women who successfully raced against her male counterparts, Pat Moss has pulled her share of wins.

The Chapins of Detroit

Part One
Roy Chapin Sr.

The young man took a deep breath, and let it out slowly. Adventure loomed before him, but there was also much to worry about. An automobile journey of this distance had never been attempted before. Some people said it couldn't be done. The gasoline automobile was a new and complicated device, notoriously unreliable. It was challenge enough to drive one on city streets, let alone the rough dirt tracks that passed for roads. And for many a stretch there would be no roads at all. There were no service stations, no network of auto repair shops, no spare parts depots. Gasoline stations were practically non-existent. Oil and gas would have to be purchased at hardware stores, and repair parts would have to be carried along. Yet here was young Roy Chapin, at the dawn of the 20th Century, about to attempt driving an automobile from Detroit, Michigan to New York City.

BY PATRICK FOSTER

Roy Dikeman Chapin was a native of Michigan, born in Lansing on February 23, 1880. His father was a prominent lawyer, and the family enjoyed a comfortable, though not lavish, standard of living. A local man, R.E. Olds, had a small shop that produced gasoline engines for stationary power plants. In 1887, Olds began experimenting with a one-cylinder gas-engine horseless carriage of his own design.

With a doting mother, sister Daisy and older brother Neil, Chapin's childhood was remembered as a very happy one. A prominent worry, however, was his health. He experienced several serious attacks of pneumonia and doctors warned against over-exertion, to the extent that his parents would not allow him to compete in athletics. He was encouraged instead to train his mind, and resting when physical activities tired him.

With the aid of scientific magazines, he built his own camera, and used it to photograph friends and neighbors, selling pictures for a small fee. It was the beginning of a lifelong love of photography.

Graduating from high school in June 1897 with no definite idea of what he wanted to do, he worked in a series of minor, low-paying jobs. Finally, in February 1899, Chapin enrolled at the University of Michigan at Ann Arbor. A boyhood chum was in the financial field in New York, and Chapin asked him to be watchful of any opportunity that

Howard Coffin

might come along.

Having started a year and a half later than others, Chapin was older and perhaps a bit more determined than most of his university classmates. He was handsome and well-dressed. Some felt him overly serious, until they saw him smile. His big, cheerful grin revealed the eager, boyish spirit that lived inside him—a spirit that would remain with him all his life. At school he met many bright young men who showed promise. But two in particular stood out. One was Howard Coffin, who had built his own workshop and regularly experimented with inventions, including a steam-powered automobile, and the other was Roscoe B. Jackson, a serious-minded young man of high intelligence.

As things turned out, Chapin's university years were cut short, but not by any offer from Wall Street. It happened when Chapin met with his former townsman R.E. Olds and then quit school to enter the new field of automobiles. He began his career at Olds Motor Works in Detroit in the Spring of 1901, when the firm was a young outfit. His duties included producing a sales catalog of the company's products.

Chapin's photography skills were also put to good use. The Olds catalog was one of the earliest in the business, and reportedly the first to use actual photos rather than car drawings. In those early days of the automobile, when high-flying promises were made about machines even before they were

produced, it was a major advantage for a car salesman to furnish photographic proof of his product. To Chapin's great joy, he was also asked to test drive cars at a small area the company had set up on Belle Isle. The situation seemed ideal.

But there were problems in the head office. Although Olds was listed as president, the company's majority stock was held by Samuel L. Smith, a wealthy investor looking to establish his two sons in business. Management, meanwhile, was split on what type of models should be offered. Smith and his sons wanted to concentrate on large, luxury cars, while Olds himself saw the greatest opportunity in offering a low-priced light automobile. The two sides clashed over the issue.

It was dramatically settled in March 1901 when a fire broke out in the Detroit plant, destroying all the prints, dies and patterns for Olds' large cars. The only product that survivied was a new light car that became known as the Curved Dash Olds.

Management feared customers would assume the Curved Dash was cheaply built, since Olds intended to introduce it with a low retail price tag of $650. For the company, it was critical to demonstrate the sturdiness and reliability of its new car in a way that would erase all doubt—what better way than an endurance run from Detroit to New York City! Such a trip had never been accomplished by an automobile, let alone by a cheaply built one. The car was planned to finish the run in time for the New York Auto Show.

The show was scheduled for early November. So, on October 27, 1901, Chapin climbed aboard the little run-

about with its stylish front section that curved up and around. A big box of spare parts was bolted behind the small seat. Motoring out of the city, he turned south and crossed into Ontario, using what few roads were available. The Olds was completely open, no top, no doors, no windshield. The faster Chapin drove in the chilly autumn air, the colder it felt, particularly at night.

Troubles soon cropped up with the cylinder gasket, which blew out on steep hills, but Chapin changed gaskets and kept on going. As the miles passed, the strain on the tiny machine began to show and other parts began to fail. An axle bent and Chapin was up all night changing it. The muddy roads were atrocious. Crossing into New York state, he ran out of roads altogether and was obliged to run his Olds on the tow paths of the old Erie Canal.

On it went, seven and a half days of open-air motoring, 860 cold miles and then finally he was there. His destination: the elegant Waldorf-Astoria on Fifth Avenue where Olds executives awaited his arrival. The ordinarily well-groomed Chapin got a rude shock, though, when the Waldorf's doorman frowned at the young man's dirty, mud-caked clothes and made him go around the back to the tradesman's entrance.

Olds executives, however, gave him a hearty welcome. Chapin was a genuine hero, a man who had attempted something bold and dangerous and had succeeded. And with his success would come Olds' success. Within days, many American newspapers had run articles about the amazing journey. Roy Chapin, 21 years old, was a national figure. People marveled at the distance, cer-

Chapin in the Curved Dash Olds

tainly, but mostly they marveled that it was done in a machine that anyone could afford to buy. At the New York Auto Show, orders flowed in. One New York dealer contracted for 1,000 cars. With orders on the books, Olds' future was secure—and so was Chapin's.

He was joined at Olds by his old university friends Howard Coffin and Roscoe Jackson, and he also became friends with Fred Bezner, who came to Olds from the National Cash Register Company. The young men shared a passion for motorcars and believed they were on the verge of extraordinary success. Chapin was named sales manager of Olds in 1904, and was said to be the youngest sales VP in the business.

He recognized his shortcomings: "I did not know a thing about territorial research; sales resistance, under that name, was an unknown quantity... We were pioneers, purely and simply. The world was our field, every man a prospect and my faith in the motorcar never wavered for an instant."

Realizing salespeople needed training in sales techniques, he studied methods used in other industries, borrowing them to write a sales manual—the first one written for the auto industry. His most important responsibility was in signing up new dealers. These came from all walks of life: operators of funeral parlors, livery stables, hardware stores—just about anyone who had cash to invest and a desire to get in on the auto industry's ground floor. One such prospect was John North Willys of Elmira, New York, who would later found his own Willys auto company. Chapin was innovative: he set a sales quota for each of his dealers. Some believe he was the first auto man to utilize quotas to increase sales volume.

But in the meantime, hard feelings between R.E. Olds and the Smiths had caused Olds to resign. One of Smith's sons was named general manager, and the company soon became a money-loser. The younger men, Chapin included, began to think about jumping ship to another company, or perhaps starting their own business. But they had no money and, because of their youth (Chapin was only 24), scant hope of securing financing.

Chapin received a handsome offer to manage the U.S. Long Distance Auto Company, but he turned it down when the owner refused to allow him to bring his friend Coffin and two others with him.

Around the same time, Coffin had come up with a design for a new car that would slot between the little Curved Dash runabout and Olds' big models. Fred Bezner, Olds purchasing agent, received the go-ahead to line up dozens of suppliers to provide components for the new car.

But the new car was canceled just weeks before production was to begin. It was the final straw. Chapin approached Coffin, Jackson, Bezner, and James Brady (rescuer of the original Runabout) with a plan to launch their own car, using Coffin's canceled design and Bezner's list of component suppliers. All but Jackson agreed to throw in their lots with Chapin. With scant personal resources, however, the group needed to find an investor who could front the estimated $200,000 needed to begin production.

His mind made up, Roy Chapin resigned from the Olds Motor Works effective March 1, 1906. He instructed his sister Daisy to pack their bags for a six-week stay in California. Since New York and Detroit banks were unwilling to back his new venture, he intended to look for money on the West Coast.

While there, he had a car dealer friend arrange a meeting with E.R. Thomas, who was then touring that part of the country. Thomas was owner of the Buffalo, New York, company that built the successful Thomas Flyer. Thomas had everything Chapin needed—money, a strong dealer network, and a respected name. The result of their meeting was the formation of a new firm called the E.R. Thomas-Detroit Company. The Thomas company in Buffalo agreed to purchase 500 of Chapin's "Thomas-Detroit" cars in the first year of production. With the agreement reached, Chapin couldn't wait to return to Michigan to begin work on the new project. Fortuitously, he and Daisy left San Francisco on April 18, 1906— mere hours before onset of the historic earthquake which devastated the city.

Issues developed on methods of getting into production, most having to do with Chapin and friends trying to raise their share of the money, but a $40,000 loan from the First and Old Detroit National Bank settled the matter. Thomas-Detroit was a success and at the end of the first year the company paid out an 80-percent dividend.

The Thomas Detroit management group, from left to right: Fred Bezner, purchasing department; James J. Brady, second vice president; Howard Coffin, vice president; Roy Chapin, general manager; and E.R. Thomas, president.

Young Chapin was the talk of the town. People said he was "good looking, very well-dressed and very serious." In July 1907 he took part in the Glidden Tour but got into trouble with police in Mishawaka, Indiana, for exceeding the speed limit of 25 miles per hour. A gentleman in all situations, he pleaded guilty and paid an $11.50 fine to the delight of the local paper, which was greatly biased against automobiles.

In its second year of production Thomas-Detroit was even more successful. Chapin, however, began to realize the drawbacks involved in the arrangement. With Thomas's dealers responsible for selling the factory's output, his little company was really just an assembler, a glorified supplier to the Buffalo firm. Once again, Chapin felt dissatisfied. His dream was to establish a company capable of engineering, building and marketing a car to its own dealers—in other words a full-fledged auto company. And because something inside continually urged him on, he couldn't rest until he reached that goal.

In 1908 he saw an opportunity when he heard that Hugh Chalmers, supercharged vice president of sales at National Cash Register, had resigned from that firm and was looking for a top position in a new industry. Chapin and friends hatched a deal whereby Chalmers bought out part of E.R.

Thomas's stake in their firm, which was renamed Chalmers-Detroit. In the new situation, company ownership was split equally in thirds among Thomas, Chalmers and Chapin and his friends. Chapin found himself, at age 28, earning nearly $50,000 per year as one-third owner of an automobile company, as well as part owner of one of the firm's suppliers. Most importantly, the company's new goal was to establish its own dealer network, and increase its sales dramatically.

Still, it wasn't long before Chapin once more grew restless. True, his share of Chalmers-Detroit gave him great affluence, but the same old fire still burned and he yearned to be the man at the helm, the one whose vision would make or break the company. It was a dream that remained just beyond his reach. Then his old friend Jackson showed up.

Roscoe B. Jackson had stayed on at Olds, even after Chapin and his friends had left. Now, though, Jackson and fellow Olds alumnus George Dunham were looking for a job, using Dunham's design for a new car as a draw. Chapin conceived the idea of putting the two to work developing three new car models, with an eye on starting a new company to produce them. Chapin and his friends would pay Jackson and Dunham out of their own private funds. On October 28, 1908, an agreement was signed that formalized the arrangement. Even Hugh Chalmers signed on as an investor. In

Roscoe Jackson

February 1909 the enterprise became a going concern. It took as its corporate title the name of an uncle of Roscoe Jackson's wife, one Joseph L. Hudson, who invested quite a lot of money in the fledgling firm. Hudson was a wealthy department store owner in the Detroit area.

The newly minted Hudson Motor Car Company was set up in a leased building on Mack Avenue in Detroit. Its prospects grew rapidly, with about 4,000 persons sending in $25 deposits to secure one of the new cars. However, for a while Chalmers-Detroit was still Chapin's primary concern—after all, the large block of stock he owned was the foundation of his wealth, so at first the new company played second fiddle in his work life. Hudson production got off to a somewhat slow start, with 1,108 cars turned out in the latter half of 1909.

By December, Chapin made a fateful decision. Although he and his friends owned a large chunk of Chalmers-Detroit, individually they were still minority owners. They yearned to own a company where they could run things the way they thought best. Deciding to bet everything they had on their ability to make Hudson a long-term success, Chapin, Bezner and Coffin sold their shares of Chalmers-Detroit to Hugh Chalmers for a whopping $788,000 cash, and bought Chalmers share of Hudson for $80,040. For better or worse, the three friends finally owned their own automobile company. Chapin was just 29 years

The Chalmers Detroit management group (top) from left to right: Roy Chapin, treasurer and general manager; Hugh Chalmers, president; E.R. Thomas, Howard Coffin, Fred Bezner and James Brady. Below: 1909 Hudson 20.

old—the youngest president of any major auto manufacturer.

In May 1910, work began on a new, vastly larger Hudson factory—designed by Albert Kahn, no less—on Detroit's Jefferson Avenue. The firm had a great year, producing some 4,508 cars, mak-

ing Chapin a millionaire at age 30.

And then came an unusual declaration. Chapin wanted to back away from the automobile business. He'd always told himself, he said, that if and when he became a millionaire, he would retire from business and devote his life to

Above: The first Hudson plant.
Left: Chapin at the wheel of a 1910 Hudson 20.

But things didn't work out the way he thought they would. Some of the young executives were not interested in owning the company, and most simply lacked the nerve to extend themselves financially to reach that goal.

Although Chapin was able to take time off for extended vacations, he was never able to walk away from the Hudson Company. Perhaps it was simply in his blood. After all, Coffin and Bezner had similar dreams and yet they were able to take life easier. Still, Chapin was living through a golden age in the auto business and he enjoyed it.

The young automaker, interested in so many diverse things, now found himself fascinated by a device altogether new and daring —the airplane. Chapin went to air shows, visited airplane manufacturers, and even looked into the possibility of Hudson producing planes. In the end, he decided against it. But he continued his interest in air travel, and became quite a flying enthusiast, meeting many of the famed aviators of the day. The Wright brothers visited him in 1909.

other things. In all likelihood, he had envisioned himself a much older man when that landmark would occur. Still, he had promised himself he would retire at the "millionaire stage," so he offered to sell controlling interest in Hudson to a group of his younger executives.

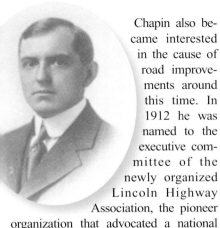

Chapin also became interested in the cause of road improvements around this time. In 1912 he was named to the executive committee of the newly organized Lincoln Highway Association, the pioneer organization that advocated a national road stretching from coast to coast. It was the beginning of another of his passions.

THE CHAPIN NAME EXTENDS

By early 1914, Chapin's friends Howard Coffin and his wife decided it might be time for the hard-working executive to take a wife, and they had a candidate in mind. She was Inez Tiedeman, daughter of the mayor of Savannah, Georgia. Lovely, educated, graceful and charming, she so impressed the Coffins that they wired Chapin to visit them right away. When he begged off, professing other plans, they good-naturedly warned him to come or consider it the last invitation he would ever receive from them. He came.

For Chapin, it was an immediate life-changing enounter. He later confessed that on the night of their initial meeting, for the first time in his life, he found it impossible to sleep.

A courtship began. At first, Inez was noncommittal. She liked Chapin, that was obvious, just as it was obvious how much he admired her. But she was just out of college, young and free, and besides, there were other admirers. Chapin wrote her constantly, sent her gifts, took every opportunity to impress her with his sincerity. His effort paid off, as they married on November 4th, 1914, in Savannah's St. John's Episcopal Church. The couple settled into a large house in the Detroit suburb of Gross Pointe Farms.

After their honeymoon, Chapin returned to work. Although Hudson sales were holding up, profitability was not growing at the same pace. The decision was made to produce more Hudson components in-house, rather than relying on costly suppliers. It was hoped that by cutting out the middleman, Hudson could price their cars lower, while at the same time increasing profit margins. Chapin introduced a new Six in mid-summer 1915, priced at a bargain $1,350, which helped spark a sales resurgence. The company ended the year placing sixth in new car registrations. Even better news came on September 21 that year, when Inez presented him with a handsome baby boy, Roy Dikeman Chapin Jr. Chapin proudly wrote to Inez's father: "This certainly is great stuff and you cannot realize what a happy family we have on Beverly Road. The Hudson Triangle is now complete."

In time, the Chapin family would be augmented by daughters Joan, Sally and Marian, and sons Jack and Dan.

In January 1916, Hudson introduced the Super-Six, a model that was to prove one of the most famous in a long line of noteworthy automobiles. At Daytona that April a Super Six set a stock car record for the measured mile, 102.5 mph, and followed up by setting a 24-hour record at Sheepshead Bay, New York. Chapin, meanwhile, made an unusual proposal in response to government efforts to tax motor vehicles and gasoline. Breaking with the no-taxes-whatsoever stance of the rest of the industry, Chapin suggested taxes levied on cars and gas be put to use to build and maintain roads. The state of America's roads was still deplorable, though somewhat improved since his historic Detroit-New York trip of '01. Chapin's proposal met favorable response and in time created huge revenues for road development.

The autumn of 1916 found Chapin volunteering more than a month of his time as an unofficial observer with Gen. John J. Pershing's motorized army, searching for the Mexican outlaw Pancho Villa.

(An interesting historical note: One night he camped at Colona Dublan, a Mormon enclave where the young George Romney—for whom Roy Jr. would one day work at American Motors—had lived the first five years of his life. Mexican revolutionaries forced the Romney family to flee to America.)

Chapin was convinced of the superiority of motor trucks over the army's horse-drawn wagons, an opinion that was shared by many when America entered the first World War in 1917; it also

Members of Hudson management in 1910 included (from top left): Fred Bezner, in charge of purchasing; Roy Chapin, president; and W.J. McAneeny, assistant to Bezner. Above: The 1916 Hudson Super Six.

1922 Essex Coach

of the Archeological Institute of America, the American Defense Society, director and president of the Detroit Symphony, member of the Court of Honor of the Boy Scouts of America and a member of the Highway Economics Committee. Roads were a special passion, and he worked tirelessly promoting highway improvements. In fact, throughout the 1920s and 1930s, Chapin was universally recognized as the leading advocate of better roads. It earned him an international reputation.

In 1921 Chapin had another new plan, the most historic of his career. He and Coffin decided to offer a closed car at a lower premium than anyone had ever tried before. The two-door Essex "Coach," provided all the closed-car comforts that wealthy people had enjoyed for years, at the low price of $1,495—only $300 more than an open touring car. The public responded enthusiastically, and Chapin knew he'd started something. By 1922 the price was reduced to $1,245, and hit its lowest point in 1925 when Chapin cut the price to $895—$5 less than the open cars.

GM's Alfred P. Sloan later recalled: "Nothing like that had ever been seen before." Chapin's close friend Edsel Ford felt the Essex Coach was Chapin's "greatest contribution to the American public and to motor travel everywhere. ... He was the first one of us to realize the public wanted a closed car if they could get it at a low price. In very little time the rest of us were concentrating on closed jobs ... but it was Roy who started it." The success of the coach model was a factor in Hudson finally building its own car bodies and was

helped in his appointment as head of the government's Highways Transport Committee. In that wartime post, he oversaw development and deployment of a vast truck operation moving goods in the United States and supplying trucks for overseas. It was an important contribution to the war effort, as well as an entirely altruistic endeavor. Because Hudson didn't build trucks, his firm received no financial benefit, and Chapin

characteristically wouldn't accept pay for his efforts; his salary was $1 a year.

When the war ended, Chapin was anxious to return to the automobile business. Hudson sales had grown over the years but Chapin was convinced that still greater volume could be acheived by adding a low-priced car to his offerings. However, he was unwilling to dilute the Hudson name. So he launched a second marque, which he dubbed the Essex. Announced on January 16, 1919, with a price tag of just $1,345, the Essex was more than just a low-priced car. Chapin's team endowed their new car with a potent four-cylinder engine that put out 55 hp, providing performance that was well above the average for an inexpensive car back then. By year end some 20,000 Essex cars had been built.

Through it all, Chapin maintained an active public service life, as a member

Left: The Hudson plant in 1930. The Essex Super Six boat-tail Speedster in 1927 (above) and 1928 (below).

probably the single most important factor in Hudson's phenomenal growth in the 1920s.

The big Hudsons, too, were enjoying fabulous years. With the introduction of low-priced coach models in the big Hudson line, sales zoomed as prices fell. By 1927 Hudson had a Standard Coach model selling for $1,285—and the company shipped 66,034 Hudsons along with a whopping 210,380 Essex cars.

In March of that year, the Chapins broke ground on a new home, a stately mansion on Lake Shore Drive in Grosse Pointe Farms. The couple spent two years studying architecture and design before deciding what style home they would build. It was a jewel, huge, breathtaking and grand, reflecting their position in society and the passions they shared.

Like many auto makers, Hudson enjoyed a peak sales year in 1929—before the effects of the Great Depression ham-

The Hudson factory showroom (above) was home to models like the 1929 Super Six dual-cowl phaeton by Biddle & Smart (below, left) and the 1931 Greater Eight (below, right).

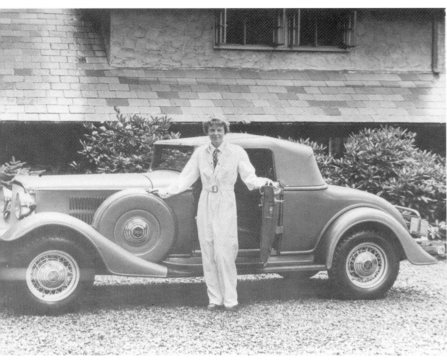

Amelia Earhart with her Terraplane.

Chapin (back, far left) with President Hoover and his Cabinet.

mered everyone—with shipments of 71,179 Hudson and 227,653 Essex automobiles, and 2,130 commercial trucks. The company made a handsome profit too, well over $11 million. That 300,962 unit total was a testimonial to the business acumen of Roy Chapin, but he would soon be tested severely in the downturn that began at the onset of 1930. And he would have to do it without many of his old friends. Howard Coffin officially retired that year. Roscoe Jackson had died the year before.

Sales collapsed overnight, with

Roy Sr., as Secretary of Commerce, with Inez.

1930's numbers coming in at less than 115,000 units. In 1931, they fell again, to just over 58,000 total. This was the era when many of America's most famous independent automakers breathed their last. Chapin struggled mightily to ensure that his firm would not end up in the boneyard. He'd been offered the job of Secretary of Commerce under President Herbert Hoover but turned it down, and later turned down the job of Under Secretary of War, explaining that in light of business conditions "it seems best to remain

at my job." Chapin was working an exhausting schedule trying to restore his company to profitability.

His solution for slow sales was a new car of extraordinary value, and Hudson men were soon working on one. Planned as a model in the Essex line, it combined a powerful six-cylinder engine with a light, short-wheelbase chassis. It would go like hell and be priced extremely low. Mindful of the country's fascination with flying machines, he named the car the Terraplane. Chapin launched it in July 1932 with an extravagant introduction. Two thousand attended, the mayor was there, the governor, Chevrolet's Bill Knudsen along with a host of other auto executives. An hour-long parade

of new Terraplanes rolled two abreast down Jefferson Avenue. The most famous aviatrix in the world, Amelia Earhart, christened the new Terraplane, and the first car off the line was given to Orville Wright.

Meanwhile, the Great Depression deepened. Unemployment rose at an unprecedented rate, and the country's economy spiraled downward. In the fourth year of his administration, President Hoover decided it was time the cabinet post of Secretary of Commerce be filled by a man with exceptional business experience. He once again called Chapin.

At first Chapin was not enthusiastic about the job. His plate was already full, with the various organizations and

Chapin boarding a '33 Terraplane, the same year that the Essex name was dropped due to poor sales.

The 1934 Terraplane helped pull Hudson from Depression-era obscurity.

committees he was involved with, his community efforts, his large family and of course his struggling car company. What more could he do?

But in the end, patriotic duty came first, and he agreed to serve in Hoover's cabinet. "It is going to be awfully hard work," he told his father-in-law, "but if I can help I want to give what I can."

He was sworn in on August 8, 1932, and immediately went to work. He attended his first cabinet meeting on August 12, and made his first general address to the country on August 22. "I am aware of the suffering our people have undergone," he said, "but looking to the future we should be able to lift

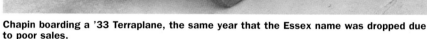

the burden of gloom and despair." He advocated a system of airports for general transportation, and felt that airmail delivery should become a permanent service of the post office. So great were his speech-making abilities that some reporters referred to him as "Hoover's orator."

The economy continued to sag. By October Chapin noted gloomily: "Commodity prices have recently shown signs of weakness, some lines of business have failed to display any rallying power and ten million persons are still out of work. We still have far to go and difficult problems to solve."

He urged the President to rethink Prohibition laws, reasoning that beer

and wine sales would provide an immediate boost to grain and agriculture markets. Hoover ignored the advice. When elections came in November, Franklin Delano Roosevelt won big, and Chapin's career as Secretary of Commerce began its final days. After Roosevelt's inauguration, Chapin and his wife returned to Detroit, where he once more assumed the presidency of The Hudson Motor Car Company.

1933 was a disastrous year for car sales. The Terraplane was about the only thing that was selling, and had so eclipsed the Essex name that Essex was dropped. Sales of big Hudsons sank so low as to be nearly non-existent. Shipments of all Hudson lines slumped to just 40,982. The company was hemorrhaging money; losses of $8.5 million were recorded in 1931 and 1932, with another $4.4 million loss for 1933. Chapin scrapped the existing line and

ordered new Hudson and Terraplane models be developed for the 1934 model year. Chapin toiled away day and night, working on plans to pull the company out of the hole it was in. In 1934 sales moved up smartly, though Hudson still lost $3.2 million. By 1935 the company was again shipping over 100,000 cars a year, and returned to profitability after a five-year drought. Unlike so many of its competitors, Hudson emerged from the Great Depression, and was ready to move ahead.

The strain Chapin went through to save the company, however, was intense. Yet he never let the stress, worry and long hours interfere with his family life. He and his oldest son, Roy Jr., spent much time fishing, golfing and playing tennis. Young Roy was devoted to his father, and nothing gave him greater pleasure than a few hours spent with his father.

The Chapin family, Roy Sr. taking Inez's right arm, Roy Jr. taking her left.

As 1936 opened, Chapin was involved in yet another great effort. He was a director of the Automotive Safety Foundation and traveled to Washington for a series of meetings regarding matters of highway traffic and safety. He wasn't feeling well, had contracted a bad cold, but felt duty-bound to honor the commitments he'd made. Upon returning to Detroit, he was still with cold.

He had a an indoor-tennis date with his old friend Edsel Ford, and thought the exercise would be beneficial. After the game, however, he felt worse. The diagnosis was pneumonia—the much-dreaded disease that had assailed him several times as a boy. It returned to strike once more. Sadly, this time it was acute. He lingered for a while but on February 16, a Sunday, he died.

Detroit's automobile community was shocked. Roy Chapin, with his boyish good looks and that wonderful smile that made you feel glad, was gone. It was one week before his 56th birthday.

Of this remarkable man, much was said. J.C. Long, a biographer, said of Chapin: "He had accomplished enough to fill several lives."

But writer Julian Street probably put it best when he stated: "He wouldn't have been the man he was ... had he not possessed that quality of eternal youth and boyishness ... and eagerness about all sorts of things." **AQ**

Don't miss the second part of the Chapin saga, an in-depth look at the contributions of Roy Chapin Jr. in the next issue of *AQ*.

NOTES AND N&C COMMENTARY

CONTACTING AQ

AQ/Automobile Quarterly, ISSN 0005-1438, is published quarterly by Automobile Heritage Publishing and Communications, LLC. Editorial and publication offices: 115 East Spring Street, Suite 102, New Albany, Indiana, USA 47150. Telephone (812) 948-AUTO (2886), fax (812) 948-2816, e-mail info@autoquarterly.com; Web site www.autoquarterly.com.

SUBSCRIPTION SERVICE

For subscriptions, back issues, indexes, reader service, changes of address, and order entry, call (866) 838-2886. If calling from Indiana or outside the U.S., call (812) 948-2886. Back issue prices start at $29.95, plus shipping. For domestic subscription orders: 1 year (4 issues), $79.95; 2 years (8 issues), $149.95; 3 years (12 issues), $199.95. For Canadian orders: 1 year, $99.95; 2 years, $189.95; 3 years, $259.95. For all other foreign orders: 1 year, $109.95; 2 years, $209.95; 3 years, $289.95. Mastercard, Visa, or American Express are accepted. Order online at www.autoquarterly.com. To order by mail, please send check or money order to **AQ/Automobile Quarterly**, 1950 Classic Car Circle, P.O. Box 1950, New Albany, IN 47151. The fax number for orders is (812) 948-2816.

POSTMASTER

Please send all changes of address to: **AQ/Automobile Quarterly**, P.O. Box 1950, New Albany, IN 47151. Periodical postage paid at New Albany, Indiana, and at additional mailing offices.

OPPORTUNITY

Details of fund raising programs for car clubs and automobile museums are available by calling: (812) 948-AUTO (2886).

Frontispiece & Contents

Color and black-and-white photography: p.1 courtesy of Stirling Moss; art pp. 2,3, courtesy of Tom Hale.

A Canadian Contribution

Special thanks to Ross Good for his wealth of insight.

Original letter (artistic rendering, p. 8) by Milton Good courtesy of Ross Good.

Art: p. 4 painting by Lance Russwurm.

Black-and-white photography: pp. 5, 9, 10, 11 AQ Photo and Research Archives.

Color photography: p. 6 AQ Photo and Research Archives; p. 7 courtesy of Ross Good; p. 9 by W.H. Heidel Photography.

James Bond Cars

Author's thanks to Ken Adam; the late John Mitchell; Margaret Rowles of the National Motor Museum, Beaulieu; Roger Stowers at Aston Martin Lagonda; and Wing-Commander Ken Wallis.

Black-and-white photography: pp. 13, 15, 16, 18 AQ Photo and Research Archives; p. 17 courtesy of Ken Adam.

Color photography: pp. 12, 14, 19 (Aston Martin), 20, 22 by Clive Friend; poster reproduction pull-outs pp. 13, 15, 16, 19, 21, 24 courtesy of AllPosters; pp. 17 (top), 23 courtesy of Eon Productions Limited, copyright National Motor Museum; pp. 17 (bottom), 21 AQ Photo and Research Archives; p. 24 courtesy of Aston Martin Lagonda; p. 25 courtesy of Ken Wallis.

Contributor David Burgess-Wise

Bodies by Saoutchik

Special thanks to Tom Solley, who has made available pictures from his great collection of sales literature published by Saoutchik from 1908 till 1939; the help and encouragement of the author's friends Laurent Friry and Alain Dollfus, both of Paris; Urs Paul Ramseier, president of the Swiss Car Register; Roger Gloor, editor at the leading Swiss periodical *Automobil Revue*; Lionel Ducrey; Christian Manz; William Morrison; Raymond Katzell; Keith Marvin; Josef Boers; and Nick Georgano.

Black-and-white photography: pp. 28 (top), 29, 30 courtesy of the Tom Solley Collection; p. 28 (bottom) from the Hediger Collection (acquired from *Auto Passion*).

Contributor Ferdinand Hediger

Color photography: pp. 26, 27 (nameplate), 33, 35, 37, 39 by Michel Zumbrunn; pp. 27 (top one and bottom two), 31 (top right and bottom), 32, 34, 36 (top left and bottom), 38 (left) from the Hediger Collection; p. 27 (second from top) from the collection of L.E. Alvarez; p. 30 courtesy of M. Karger, Great Britain; p. 31 (top left) copyright Bobbie'dine Rodda; p. 36 (top right) courtesy of Nick Georgano; p. 38 (right) courtesy of Christian Manz.

Bibliography

The Golden Age of the Luxury Car; A History of Coachbuilding; Catalogue des Catalogues (various years); *Les voitures de luxe des années 50; Klassische Wagen 1919-1939; Mercedes-Benz Personenwagen 1886-1984; Les plus belles voitures du monde; Coupé; Klassiche Cabriolets; 100 of the World's Finest Automobiles*

Many magazines were consulted, among them: *Automobile Quarterly, Automobil Revue (CH), Auto Carrosserie (F), La Vie Automobile (F), Omnia (F), L'Enthousiaste (F), Fanatique de l'Automobile (F), Automobiles Classiques (F), Motor Trend, L'Illustration (F), Réalités (F),* and *L'Equipement Automobile (F)*

Art Gallery

All original art and information provided by automotive artist Tom Hale.

Route 66

Special thanks to James Powell of the Missouri Route 66 Association and the assistance of Paul Taylor, founding editor of *Route 66 Magazine*. Thanks also to the many local and regional organizations who have kept the legend and legacy of Route 66 alive—the highway is truly a significant and living part of Amercian heritage.

Black-and-white photography: pp. 52, 54 (of Avery) AQ Photo and Research Archives; p. 54 (strip map) courtesy of James Powell; pp. 55, 56, 58, 59 courtesy of *Route 66 Magazine*.

Color photography: pp. 50, 52, 57, 60, 61 by Carolyn Hasofratz; p. 54 courtesy of *Route 66 Magazine*.

Bibliography

James E. Cook quote: *Route 66 Remembered*, by Michael Karl Witzel (Motorbooks, 1996). Also quoted: "Our Gastronomic Highways," *House & Garden*, December, 1923; "Route 66 Straight Ahead," *The New Republic*, August 6, 1956.

Works consulted: *Route 66, Photographic Essay* by Quinta Scott, text by Susan Croce Kelly (University of Oklahoma, 1988); *Route 66: The Mother Road*, by Michael Wallis, (St. Martin's, 1990); *Four Great Highways From Sea to Sea*, Literary Digest, May 26, 1923; "Unfit for Modern Motor Traffic," *Fortune*, August 1936; "Motoring at 100 mph," *Business Week*, September 9, 1939; "U.S. 66—Big Swing to the Coast," *Better Homes & Gardens*, March, 1955; "Route 66 Boulevard to the Golden West," by Harris Edward Dark, *Today's Health*, June 1963.

Related Clubs

National Historic Route 66 Federation
P.O. Box 423, Dept. WS
Tunjunga, CA 91043-0423
Ph./Fax: (818) 352-7232
national66@national66.org

Route 66 International Association
2700 S. Kiowa
Lake Havasu City, AZ 86403
Ph.: (520) 680-6677
Fax: (520) 453-2288
route66@ctaz.com

National Automobile Museum

Appreciation is extended to the following for their assistance in preparing this article:

Contributor Kathy Berry

Jackie Frady, executive director of the museum; and Summer Kay, education and

museum services manager.

Black-and-white photography: pp. 65, 67, 69 AQ Photo and Research Archives.

Color photography: pp. 62, 63, 64, 66, 67 (top and bottom left), 68-73 from the National Automobile Museum; p. 67 (right-hand collage) AQ Photo and Research Archives.

Contact Information
National Automobile Museum
10 Lake Street South
Reno, Nevada 89501
Ph.: (775) 333-9300
Hours: 9:30 a.m.-5:30 p.m., Monday-Saturday; 10:00 a.m.-4:00 p.m., Sunday
www.automuseum.org

Stirling Moss

A world of gratitude goes out to the man himself, Sir Stirling Moss, for his uncompromised accommodation in the preparation of this article, as well as the trailing "sidebar" on his family's racing tradition. The editors wish to express their appreciation, as well as admiration, for him.

All black-and-white photography courtesy of Stirling Moss.

Bibliography
Stirling Moss: The Authorised Biography by Robert Edwards;
Stirling Moss's Motor-Racing Masterpieces by Stirling Moss (with Christopher Hilton);
Stirling Moss: My Cars, My Career by Stirling Moss (with Doug Nye)

Moss Family Racing Tradition
All black-and-white photography courtesy of Stirling Moss.

Roy Chapin, Sr.
The author wishes to thank Bill Chapin and all of the Chapin family for their help in preparing this article and providing photos.

All black-and-white photography courtesy of Bill Chapin.

All color photography from the AQ Photo and Research Archives.

Contributor Patrick Foster

Bibliography
Recognition is given to some of the sources used in writing this article:
The excellent biography Roy D. Chapin, (1945) by J.C. Long, was a primary resource.
Other books consulted were:
Automotive Giants of America (1926) by Forbes and Foster;
The Story of the Hudson Motor Car 1909-1957 (1975) by Mitch and Ted Mayborn;
Automobile Quarterly Vol. IX Number 4.

Notes & Commentary
Color photography p. 111 courtesy of Sterling Publishing Co., Inc.

Coda
Color photography courtesy of Stirling Moss.

Back Cover
Debossment of Stirling Moss's signature from the AQ Photo and Research Archives.

Stirling Moss's accomplishments in a racing car—any type of racing car—bordered on the incredible. A top driver once remarked after being beaten by Moss, "I wouldn't mind losing to him if he was a normal human being. He's just too much."

A genius behind the steering wheel, Moss's life and times are brilliantly recorded by Robert Edwards in his new book "Stirling Moss: The Authorized Biography." Edwards is the first writer to have full access to the family files and photographs, and he makes good use of this privilege.

Edwards begins with a history of the Moss family on both sides (they date back to the 1400s) and closes with Sir Stirling today. Knighted in 2000, Moss, now 71, still keeps busy in public relations and historic car racing.

Along with history and family tales, everything about Moss is here —including his famous Mille Miglia victory in 1955 with his friend Denis Jenkinson; his admiration for Argentine world champion and Mercedes teammate Juan Manuel Fangio; and his beating the entire three-car factory Ferrari team at the Grand Prix of Monaco in 1961 while driving a privately entered, year-old RobWalker Lotus.

Moss loved playing the role of the underdog, and the book tells why. Playing this role made him even more popular — both in Britain and the rest of the world.

From his first race in 1948 until his near fatal crash in a Lotus in 1962, his fascinating and dangerous life unfolds in great detail. Superb action photos, many in color, vividly support the text.

This book comes highly recommended to admirers of Stirling Moss and also to those who admire the racing era of the 1950s and early '60s.

—Randy Barnett

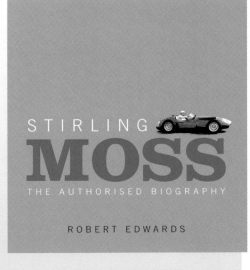

STIRLING MOSS
THE AUTHORISED BIOGRAPHY

ROBERT EDWARDS

"Stirling Moss: The Authorised Biography" by Robert Edwards
Price: $45.00 (Canada $67.50)
ISBN: 0-304-35904-1
Hardcover, 360 pages
To order, contact:
Sterling Publishing Co., Inc.
(800) 805-5489

the Maserati offered Stirling the opportunity to refine his style

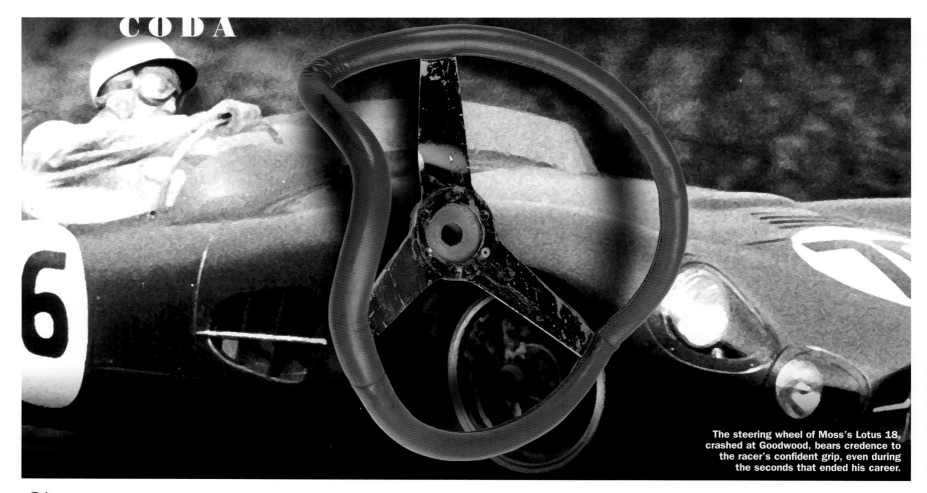

CODA

The steering wheel of Moss's Lotus 18, crashed at Goodwood, bears credence to the racer's confident grip, even during the seconds that ended his career.

Stirling Moss, indeed, lived and worked in the fast lane. He did it all in the world of motorsport, and what better way to punctuate our tribute than with views from some of those who raced with him and witnessed his feats on the track. ▲◉

"It is well said that Stirling could win in a wheelbarrow."
—Rob Walker, wealthy British private entrant for whom Moss scored some of his greatest victories

"Moss stood head and shoulders above his contemporaries in the grand prix world and his drive to win the Mille Miglia in 1955 is unparalleled. He did things with a car that other drivers could not believe. Roy Salvadori told me that he (Roy) would think as Moss went by: 'Oh, really now Stirling, that's just not possible.'"
—Cameron Argetsinger, the man who was primarily responsible for establishing Watkins Glen as a U.S. Grand Prix racing site

"No other post-war driver, arguably bar the supreme Argentinian, has proved greater, and certainly none who could approach Stirling's demonstrable class—Jimmy Clark or Jackie Stewart —could match either his inclination or his ability to perform so majestically (and with such dedicated frequency) in such a bewildering diversity of cars."
—Doug Nye, racing journalist and historian

"It is not without reason that they call you 'The Champion without a crown.'"
—Juan Manuel Fangio